The Optimist's Guide
to Finland

Russell Snyder

Entertaining and enlightening. Generously sprinkled with humor. Full of inspiring illustrations.

The Optimist's Guide
to Finland

Russell Snyder

Illustrations: Maija Raitanen

A guide to the culture, customs and business life of Finland.

Facts, essentials, and practical advice. Plus, anecdotes, observations and personal stories from a foreign resident who has lived and experienced Finland for over twenty years – and enjoyed it.

YRITYSKIRJAT OY

SURVIVAL GUIDES

Author: Russell Snyder
Illustrations and layout: Maija Raitanen

© Copyright: YRITYSKIRJAT OY & Russell Snyder

Published by YRITYSKIRJAT OY, Helsinki, Finland
Internet: www.yrityskirjat.fi
E-mail: kirjat@yrityskirjat.fi

Printed at Gummerus Printing Jyväskylä, Finland 2003
1 st Edition

ISBN: 952-9660-45-6

CONTENTS

Introduction

My father is to blame for introducing me to Finland. His favorite composer is Sibelius, and I still remember the time when *"Finlandia"* was playing on his old phonograph. He said, "Finland must be an exceptional country to produce a genius like Sibelius." My father also admired Paavo Nurmi, the legendary runner.

When I was ten years old, Mrs. Tyler, my teacher, spoke enthusiastically to us about Finland. It was one of the rare occasions when I was actually paying attention in class and I heard her say, "This is a brave, little country that has had to fight so many times for its freedom. We could all learn something from the Finns."

During my later school years, I met kids with names like Jarvi, Maki, or Lahti who proudly told me they were "Finnish." When I asked them what Finland was like, I would get a

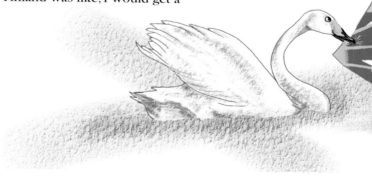

disappointing reply like, "How should I know, I've never been there."

It wasn't until I came over to Europe that I met *real* Finns. I generally found them to be unpretentious and friendly. They always seemed happy to talk about their country. Not in a bragging way, but with a natural and genuine affection for the place. It was because of these cordial, traveling Finns that I decided to see for myself what this land was really like.

Arriving in Helsinki in 1973 via the charming port of Turku, I wandered around town until my feet hurt. I didn't use a map, I just kept my eyes and ears open, taking in the seascapes, the greenery and the sights. This, indeed, was a pleasant city. I felt good here. Then I traveled around the countryside by train. People were easy to meet and hospitable (of course, it was summer) and the scenery was extraordinary. After that trip, the images and memories of Finland stayed in my mind and I knew I would have to come back. And after returning several times to visit other parts of the country, I made a monumental decision. In the summer of 1982, I arrived in Finland for a one-year's stay. Well... I'm still here.

I had many positive experiences during my first year in Finland. A weekend on an island in the middle of the world's most beautiful archipelago. Picnics with friends in the middle of pristine forests. A swim in a lake at midnight. A stroll on a country path during a spectacular sunset in early autumn. Dancing in a small town restaurant until closing time and going with half the patrons to someone's house for an after-hours party. Operas, classical music concerts, ballets, folk music recitals, and festive dinners. Cross-country skiing over hills and across frozen lakes. I could go on and on, but I think you get the picture and probably understand why I stayed here.

This book is a guide to Finnish culture, customs and business life. I don't want to simply give you facts and figures, I want to provide you with a sense of what it is like to visit, travel, live and work here. I hope to give you an idea of why Finland is like it is, and why the Finns are like they are. Perhaps you will find this country as captivating, delightful, charming and even puzzling as I do. Most of all, though, I would like to motivate you to discover as much as you can about Finland. And, like many previous visitors, you may find that one trip is not enough, and you'll be compelled to come back for more. So along with the practical information, there are anecdotes, observations and personal stories.

By the way, my father has now fulfilled his dream and visited Finland several times. "It is an exceptional place," he told me after attending a Sibelius concert at the Sibelius Academy... which is located near a statue of Paavo Nurmi.

Tervetuloa – Welcome

Russell Snyder

*The first records of man in Finland date back to around
9000 B.C.*

A Two-Minute History of Finland

The Finns have ice to thank for the present day beauty of their country. During the last ice age, glaciers (must have been artistic ones) carved out the thousands of lakes, hills, fells, and islands around Finland. The glaciers melted around 10000 B.C. and soon after that, potential homeowners looking for bargains started moving in. The first records of man in Finland date back to around 9000 B.C. Archeologists know this because they found stone weights, bark floats and antler carvings, which were either important artifacts or just stuff that the Mesolithic people were throwing away.

Around 3000 B.C., *Finno-Ugric* people from the Ural Mountains on their way to Hungary or Florida, apparently got lost and settled in Finland instead – they didn't seem to notice the difference, though. There were also Vikings and

Northern European tribesmen who came to Finland, either for the fantastic fishing and hunting opportunities or because they weren't welcome anyplace else. Meanwhile, the *Proto-Sami* people who had been living here since 6000 B.C. thought the place was getting too crowded and moved up north.

In the 12th century, Sweden was looking for a new place to conquer that didn't have a large army. In 1155 A.D. the Swedes came over to Finland on religious crusades. They liked the place so much that they decided to add it to the Swedish Empire. The reaction among the Finns was mixed. Some fought furiously against the invaders, while others thought: Well, this could be an excellent opportunity to practice Swedish.

The Swedes set up Turku as the Finnish capital and built castles, towns, schools, churches and manors around the country. They constructed roads, iron-works, paper mills and fortresses. Finns worked on Swedish-owned land, served in the Swedish army and listened politely to lots of boring Swedish speeches. The Swedish rule has had a lasting impression on Finland, and even today, Finns still love meatballs, sing loads of Swedish drinking songs at formal parties, and are obsessed with being on time.

Russia had its eye (or, according the double eagle symbol, two of its four eyes) on Finland for a long time. In 1809, after several wars, they kicked the Swedes out. The Russians moved the capital to Helsinki and Finland became an autonomous Grand Duchy of the Russian Empire. During this period, the Finns were allowed to have their own senate, post office, customs office, currency, and railroads. Finnish became an official language along with Swedish. Understandably with all these new freedoms, the Finns wanted more. Writers, artists and musicians noticed that all they needed to do was produce a work with independence as a theme and it would become a big hit.

In 1917, to put it mildly, Russia had some problems. In fact, not only were they doing badly in World War I, they had a couple of revolutions to boot. Finland perceived this as the silver lining of a dark cloud and declared independence. The new Russian rulers, the Bolsheviks, agreed to this declaration, hoping Finland would see the light and join the new Soviet Union. Finland, instead, chose to go its own way, and even selected a king, Prince Friedrich Karl of Hessen, Germany. He resigned after only

It was a devastating conflict and after a short but cruel struggle, the Whites, under the command of Mannerheim, were victorious.

three months, though, because Germany lost the war (his crown and throne still exist, by the way).

However, all was not well in Finland. The socialist "Reds" had their heart set on building a socialist paradise together with their Soviet neighbors, so they staged a coup. The government "White" forces fled the capital and a civil war broke out. It was a devastating conflict and after a short but cruel struggle, the Whites, under the command of Mannerheim, were victorious. Nonetheless, the price of victory was high: 30,000 dead, numerous executions and mistrust that lasted for many years. Finland became a republic and K.J. Ståhlberg was elected Finland's first president.

Many challenges faced the new republic. They had to maintain peace with their unpredictable neighbors, the Soviets; they had to ensure an adequate food supply produced in difficult farming conditions; and they had to contain the spread of fascist political groups such as the *Lapua movement*. In the face of these difficulties, Finland improved its economy, increased exports, excelled in many sports, introduced the world to "Finnish design," and invented their own version of the tango.

In 1939 the Soviet Union and Germany secretly signed a pact that effectively divided up Europe between the two powers. According to the pact, Finland fell under jurisdiction of the Soviet Union and the Soviets demanded to put military bases there. Finland didn't agree with this idea and said, *"Njet."* An infuriated Soviet Union sent a large, well-equipped force to conquer paltry Finland, but they were totally unprepared for the worst winter in years. The Soviets were stunned by the fierce, Finnish soldiers who dressed in white, donned skis and maneuvered with prowess through the snowy forests. Finland didn't technically win the Winter War, but they amazingly

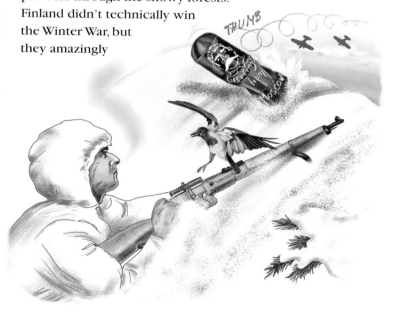

kept their sovereignty and signed an interim peace treaty in 1940.

Then Germany suddenly turned against the Soviet Union. Finland took this opportunity to get assistance from the Germans in support of its fight against the Soviets and became limited allies with them. This Continuation War (World War II) lasted from 1941 to 1944. Finland fought bravely and boldly, but in the end there were simply too many Soviet troops with too much military equipment. Finland was forced to sign an unfavorable treaty to save its hide. It had to forcibly remove the German troops stationed in Lapland (who didn't really want to leave), it had to cede Petsamo in the north and large areas of Karelia, and pay $300,000,000 (a considerable sum in those days) in reparations.

With legendary effort, the Finns chased the 200,000 German soldiers from Lapland, evacuated 450,000 Karelians and resettled them, and started building up industries in order to pay off the reparations. Altogether, 90,000 Finnish men lost their lives in the war and many more suffered physical wounds and psychological trauma from those terrible years. Fortunately, Finland retained its sovereignty and independence. Later, literature about the Winter War and Continuation War became popular reading and some works were even turned into films and plays. The most famous example is, "The Unknown Solder," by Väinö Linna.

After the war Finland was preoccupied with having a good relationship with the west, while keeping the Soviets from making any surprise visits with their army. This might be compared to walking a tightrope. In 1948 President J.K.

Paasikivi signed the Treaty of Friendship, Cooperation and Mutual Assistance, which was often criticized in the west but succeeded at keeping any Soviet aggression at bay.

The Cold War was soon in full swing and Finland was under pressure from the Soviets not to accept Marshall aid. So they continued to use all the resources they could muster and developed industrial output in order to pay off debts. Finally, in 1952 the last payment was made. During the same year the Finns were hosting the Olympics, drinking their first Coca Colas, and celebrating Armi Kuusela's Miss Universe title. In 1955 Finland joined the United Nations and was now privileged to take part in the endless, longwinded discussions.

The legendary Urho Kekkonen became president in 1956 and he basically continued Paasikivi's policies and added some of his own. He managed to stay in that high office for a record 25 years, although some suspect he wasn't quite with it the last couple of years. Kekkonen was, among other things, a champion of diplomacy. He was credited with finding solutions to difficult problems by taking politicians into his personal sauna for undisturbed

Kekkonen's self-portrait "PEEL"

and candid dialogue. One of the most significant events during this period was the 1975 Conference on Security and Cooperation in Europe that took place in Helsinki. The secure atmosphere of Finland allowed world leaders to argue and yell at each other in peace.

Finland voted to join the European Union in 1994 and sailed into the European bureaucratic sea in 1995. The European presidency was held by Finland in 1999, and as an additional honor, Helsinki was chosen as one of the Cultural Capitals of Europe in 2000. Also in 2000, Tarja Halonen was elected as Finland's first woman president. In 2002 the Euro became the only official currency to be used in Finland. Good-bye Finnish mark.

Economically Speaking

Finland has been doing business for thousands of years. At first the primitive inhabitants traded such primitive items as raw timber, dried fish, elk meat and primitive jewelry (which has recently come back into fashion for a very modern price). In later centuries tar making became a very profitable enterprise (albeit a messy one), as did the production of sawn wood, paper and iron. Finland steadily developed its industries during the Swedish, Russian and early independence periods, but at a much slower pace than the rest of Europe. Consequently, even up until the 1950s, the country remained a predominantly agrarian society – with a somewhat limited selection of fine restaurants, first-rate theaters and haute couture.

At the end of World War II Finland agreed to pay the Soviet Union massive reparations in the form of manufactured goods. Then to make things worse, the Soviets gave them such a poor exchange rate, that it effectively doubled the amount of debt. To meet this obligation, Finland had to frantically modernize and expand its existing industries, and establish many new ones. The schedule of payments was virtually impossible, but it was either that, or start speaking Russian and eating borscht soup. So the government made large investments, inventers came up with new ideas, managers ensured productivity, workers labored diligently and people started drinking a lot of strong coffee.

According to the agreement, Finland had to send the Soviet Union goods that comprised 70% metal products such as machinery, ships, locomotives, and electrical cables. They also sent wood products, textiles, shoes and anything else the Soviets were interested in, which was basically everything. By the time the last payment had been made in 1952, the Soviet Union was hooked on Finnish goods and was ready to buy them, but not for cash. Finland kept the products flowing east and the Soviets paid for them in the form of oil, other raw materials and sometimes canned borscht soup.

That's how the rural Finland of farmers went through the fastest process of industrialization and urbanization in European history. The Finns not only maintained a steady market in the USSR, they also built up lucrative trade with the west. A post-war economic miracle was achieved and Finland began to prosper. Now they could afford deluxe coffee.

The 1970s and 80s were boom years in Finland. Unemployment was low and salaries were high. It was a time of easy bank loans, and credit was given to almost anyone who asked for it. People were getting rid of money as fast as they got it, and inflation soared like an eagle.

By the end of the 1980s Finland was one of the most expensive countries in the world. The Finns ended up losing their competitive edge in the west, but they didn't mind too much because the Soviet Union was ready to buy almost anything Finland could turn out.

Then reality hit. The Soviet Union disintegrated at the beginning of the 1990s, which cost Finland 25% of its export market. Combine that with a worldwide economic decline and poor investments by Finnish companies and banks, and you have quite a recession. The Finnish stock market dropped like a lead balloon, unemployment figures rose like a skyrocket, companies died like flies, debts piled up like horse manure and people had to find inexpensive hobbies like sleeping. On the positive side, prices sank and Finland became one of the cheapest countries in Europe.

Some pessimists called this recession a "depression" because, at its worst, unemployment reached a whopping 20%. In response to this situation the Finnish government

cut domestic spending and limited labor costs. It worked closely with the private sector, yet still maintained strong social welfare benefits, which was quite a juggling act. By the mid-1990s gross domestic product rose significantly and the stock market was at a higher level than before the recession.

Exports have been at the forefront of the Finnish recovery. There is an old proverb that Finland lives on her forests and this is still true today. Paper, pulp, wood and board production make up Finland's second largest export sector. The third largest source of exports comes from the metal and engineering sector. Finland produces and exports basic metals such as steel, zinc, copper and nickel. However, advanced machinery and equipment make up the biggest share of metals exports.

It was once said that Finnish exports stand on two legs, one wooden and one metal. But now a third, larger leg has developed: Electronics and telecommunications. This sector has expanded rapidly in recent years and now makes up the largest percentage of exports. Finland puts a premium on research and development, and this has helped it become one of the world's top technology countries. Of course, Nokia is the best-known success story in Finland, but many other high-tech companies have made their mark as well. Additional Finnish exports include chemicals, scientific equipment, high-quality textiles, designed household items and processed foods.

State companies have played a vital role in the post-war economy. Without state investments Finland wouldn't have been able to build up its industry and pay off its heavy war

It was once said that
Finnish exports stand on
two legs, one wooden
and one metal. But now
a third, larger leg has
developed: Electronics
and telecommunications.

reparations. In recent years, because of economic pressures, international competition and policy within the European Union, Finland has been gradually selling off its holdings. This strategy of privatization will continue at a steady pace so long as the state can get a decent price for its shares. After all, we all (including the government) want to make a nice profit.

Taxation is a common topic of conversation among Finnish business circles. There are various taxes on profits, VAT, stamp duties, license fees, import and customs duties – plus the state and local authorities seem to add something new whenever they can get away with it. On the other hand, Finns now enjoy a great deal of social programs such as generous maternity/paternity leave, financial allowances for families, public health care, unemployment benefits, and a state retirement plan. The present government has promised to reform and reduce taxes, and with pressure from the European Union and other economic organizations, I believe they really will.

Minding Finnish Business

A number of factors make Finland a good place to do business. It is ideally situated between the stable and strong economies of Scandinavia and the emerging markets of the East. Finns are known to be hard workers and honest businesspeople. Moreover, they are eager to buy and sell, and will give you straightforward answers about their products and services.

Foreign businesspeople will find that Finnish hosts are friendly and often fluent in several languages. Although they don't have a reputation of being skilled in the art of

Finns like to entertain their guests with sightseeing.

small talk, they are attentive and good listeners. You can talk to them about many subjects. Finns take pride in their knowledge of world politics, the economy and geography. They read the newspaper, listen to radio reports, watch the news on TV and can discuss current events from various angles. However, it is often up to the guest to get the conversation going and to maintain it with intelligent questions because in the Finnish culture, silence is perfectly acceptable.

It is commonplace for Finns to entertain their guests with sightseeing, a visit to the sauna, a meal in a fine restaurant, a classical music concert, an evening of drinking and dancing at a night club, or a day at a picturesque cottage. Usually their company provides an adequate expense account for these activities.

Finnish businesspeople are generally diligent and meticulous, even though they enjoy lots of holiday time. Finland is not considered a religious country but Finns still adhere to the protestant work ethic. They like shaking hands, exchanging business cards (they usually have an English version) and swapping dry humor (if they tell a joke about Finland, it would be amiable to come back with a tasteful joke about your own country). They are modest, prompt and expect others to be on time – not too early and definitely not too late. Since Finnish businessmen are not the most spontaneous of people, it is usually necessary to make an appointment in advance if you want to meet somebody. If you don't know the person, this is best accomplished through a secretary. You might find that some Finns are more eager to communicate by phone than in person. And sometimes you might find that they are more eager to communicate by email or fax than by phone. Don't worry, at least you are communicating, so make sure you use the phone/fax/email to the best of your ability.

In the past Finns had a reputation for being industrious individualists, but nowadays, within companies, teamwork and team spirit are being emphasized. The hierarchy is not as pronounced at Finnish work places as in many other countries, and at most companies employees are able to get access to all or most levels of management. Employees are encouraged to openly express their views and supervisors will listen. In contrast to Sweden, however, consensus is not vital and the boss makes the final decisions.

At business meetings coffee, tea and pastries are served in abundance no matter what time of day it is, often accompanied by juice, sandwiches, and canapés. When lunch meetings are called for, they are often held in the company restaurant if there is one. Alcoholic beverages are not served in this kind of business atmosphere, but, of course, there are exceptions. Finns take a no nonsense approach to meetings and they follow the agenda as closely as possible. Things usually go smoothly and efficiently, often the important decisions have been made in advance.

When it comes to negotiations, Finns like to get straight to the point. In this country of engineer-dominated management, facts are more important in a presentation than pizzazz. If you want to sell something you need to know the technical details of your product well. You have to be able to answer questions and supply the relevant data. But don't panic, take your time, Finns have lots of patience.

Don't expect lots of questions, though, Finns will ask something only if they didn't understand or if they need more information to make a decision.

Although there is usually room for maneuvering, Finns don't like long bargaining sessions. A friendly handshake signifies a deal has been made and you can normally count of a Finn to keep up his end. Traditionally, the signing of the contract was seen as just a formality. However, as members of the European Union, Finns have now placed more importance on carefully written agreements.

Not big followers of fashion (although, Finland has a healthy number of fashion designers), Finns tend to dress casually whenever possible.

Sometimes they will joke that the Finnish national costume is a jogging suit. Nonetheless, in business situations, both men and women are inclined to dress

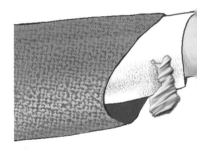

conservatively. Less formally in IT and high tech firms, more formally in traditional businesses. For festive occasions men like to wear dark suits or dinner jackets and women often go all out to be stylish.

By all means give business gifts. They should generally be small and shouldn't be seen as a bribe or an inducement. Something from your company, a tasteful souvenir from your country, a coffee table book or a bottle of wine would certainly be appreciated.

You will always make a good impression by showing your Finnish hosts that you know something about their country. Throw out a few facts, historical events and famous names wherever possible. Try out a few polite Finnish greetings and expressions. Your efforts, no matter how modest, will be valued. And remember, feel free to ask lots of questions, because Finns love talking about their country.

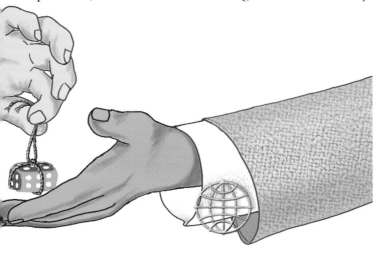

A Well-Managed Wilderness

*J*ohan Snellman, a distinguished writer and statesman of the 19th century, believed Finland's forests should all be felled. He proposed that profits from the lumber could be used to develop agriculture and thereby bring Finland into the civilized world. Fortunately, not everybody wanted that kind of civilization and Snellman's ideas were not employed. Today, Finland remains the world's most forested country. The woodlands not only bring in vast material wealth, they provide immeasurable spiritual richness and unlimited recreational opportunities. What's more, the forest reserves are greater now than they were during the last century, and they continue to grow.

Ancient Finns depended on the forest to supply them with game, firewood, berries and other woodland bounty. Hunters needed to stay in the good graces of Tapio, the god of the forest, before setting out to find dinner.

Later, during the boom years of shipbuilding, wood tar was in great demand by the industrial countries of Europe. Finland gained great prosperity making and exporting tar from the 17th to the 19th century. Unfortunately, the tar business took a great downturn when steel ships came into vogue. However, Finland continued to develop its forest industry by employing legions of lumberjacks, erecting sawmills and transporting logs by water. Nowadays, a considerable share of Finland's prosperity comes from the export of sawn wood, pulp, paper, plywood, particleboard as well as furniture, saunas, doors and log cabins.

Forests cover around 70% of the land, making trees Finland's most important natural resource. Pine, spruce and birch are the most commercially exploited trees, but aspen, alder, rowan, larch, juniper and common ash are also cultivated. Surprisingly, about three-quarters of the forests are owned by ordinary, private citizens. Forestry is an essential source of income for many families and communities.

It is in everybody's interest to maintain healthy forests. For that reason trees are carefully managed, harvested and replanted. Already in 1886 a law was passed forbidding the wasteful use of forest resources. All landowners are under legal obligation to replace anything they cut down. This law continues to be updated and augmented with new and pertinent regulations. Currently, the authorities are not only concerned with renewable resources, they are also trying to ensure biodiversity in the nation's wilderness areas.

When it comes to forestry know-how, Finland is at the forefront. It manufactures extremely advanced, state-of-the-art-harvesters, paper and packaging board machines, machinery for producing sawn goods, pulp processing and finishing machines, plus related chemicals, automation and control systems. If you ever need anything for your country's forestry industry, Finland has it. Furthermore, this is one of the best places to study forestry for either practical application or for a university degree.

The Finnish wilderness is not just about industrial production, it provides a vital source of recreation for the population. This is an ideal environment for walking, trekking, camping, fishing, hunting, and for those in top condition, rock climbing and orienteering. In winter the forests host masses of skiers representing all levels of ability.

A law called "Everyman's Right" allows people to roam freely on foot, bicycle or skis (but not by motor vehicle), and enjoy nature's bounty in any forest, whether private or public. Everyone is free to pick delicious lingonberries, blueberries, wild strawberries, or, succulent mushrooms such as chanterelles, boletus, and milk caps. You may even sell them tax-free if you choose. You can also pick wild flowers to your heart's delight. Special permission is needed, though, for fishing, hunting or building a campfire.

Sometimes the forest is called a Finn's church. Probably because it is the place where one can escape from the stresses of everyday life, relax and reenergize. Walking on a carpet of pine needles, listening to the birds and insects, inhaling the fragrances of the woods, sensing a fresh breeze on the face, watching sunbeams stream through the branches, and contemplating a trickling stream help take the mind off worries. Artists, writers, and musicians come to the wilderness to seek inspiration. Nature lovers and biologists come to encounter some of the thousands of plant varieties, mosses and lichens. Bird watchers and ornithologists can observe more than 350 wild birds. Animal enthusiasts can regard deer, beavers, wolverines, and elk in their natural habitat. Photographers can track some of the rarer species such as wolves, eagles, and lynx. And provided you don't get too close to an elk, or between a bear and food, or step on a viper, or get bitten by a disease-carrying tick, or get caught in subzero weather without the right clothing, or get lost... there is nothing to worry about in the Finnish forest.

The Kivinen Family

At 35, Kari Kivinen has already achieved excellence in marketing at 3 different high tech firms. Although people think of Finnish engineers as being taciturn, he is very outgoing and a natural salesman. Presently, Kari is the marketing director of a company specializing in scientific measuring devices. He often puts in long days, and if something needs to be taken care of, he won't hesitate to work during the weekend.

Katariina, his wife, is an accountant. She has remained at the same bank since graduation, even though the bank has merged and changed names three times. Katariina has incredible powers of concentration and is appreciated for her meticulous and thorough work. Last year she became department supervisor. Unlike Kari, she is quiet and reserved. She seems more confident around facts and figures than around people.

Kari and Katariina met while they were students. He studied electrical engineering at the University of

Technology and she studied accounting at the Helsinki School of Economics. One evening Katariina went with her friends to the opera. After the performance they decided to have a glass of wine at a bar. Five bars and five glasses of wine later Katariina spotted a tall, blond, and self-confident man. The man of her dreams. Fortified with liquid courage she struck up a conversation with him. In fact they chatted for three hours before Katariina's friends finally dragged her home.

The image of that petite, black-haired beauty he'd met the other night really stayed in his mind. When he called her several days later she sounded different, though: timid and embarrassed. She seemed reluctant to get together at first but finally agreed to meet him. They ended up hitting it off over a delightful meal of seafood dishes in a cozy restaurant. He did most of the talking and she was an enthusiastic listener. Soon they were seeing each other several times a week. Six months later they moved in together.

Nowadays, the Kivinens live in the city of Espoo in a modern and comfortable house. They like the neighborhood and are happy with the school their son, Kalle, is attending. There is even space for Kari to wash and wax his new BMW. He is really proud of that car and can't understand why Katariina hangs on to her old Toyota. Kari likes to have fine things: name-brand clothes, designed furniture, vintage wines, expensive cigars, and gourmet foods. Katariina, on the other hand, has modest tastes and believes in simple pleasures. She is frugal with her money. But she understands her husband. He grew up in a poor family in

Eastern Finland on rustic food, hand-me-down clothes and very few toys. Now he has money to burn. The funny thing is, Katariina finds that Kari's parents are two of the happiest people she has ever met.

Kalle is 10 years old and a typical schoolboy. The way Kari plies his son with toys and gadgets you'd think he would be spoiled. But neighbors and teachers all comment on how good natured and polite the boy is. Katariina worries about his latest hobby, though. Ever since Kari bought him a guitar, Kalle spends a great deal of his free time practicing. "I want to be in a famous band like The Rasmus and HIM. I'm going to have a hit record someday." That reminds Katariina of the time she dreamed of playing the kantele in a Finnish folkdance group. She still plays it now and then. It reminds Kari of the time he wanted to be clarinet player in a jazz band. His clarinet has been gathering dust in the closet for years.

Education is important to the Kivinen Family. Both Kari and Katariina frequently attend job-sponsored seminars and workshops. In addition to that, Kari takes a Chinese language course on Monday nights because China is an important market for his company. Katariina goes to an Italian cooking course on Tuesday nights because she doesn't want to think about her job after working hours. Kalle attends a computer club on Wednesday afternoons because he wants to surf the internet more efficiently.

During the last few years, Kari has noticed that the number on his bathroom scale has been rising. Maybe it's because of all the business entertaining he does in restaurants. He has started doing Nordic pole walking three times a week and plays soccer on Sundays. "You put on more calories in the after-match beer drinking than you burn off playing the game," Katariina points out. Her fitness program consists of an aerobics and weight training class three times a week. However, she doesn't mention the rich pastries and double cappuccino she takes later. Kalle plays pesäpallo (Finnish baseball) in the summer, ice hockey during winter and basketball all year long. Like most Finns the Kivinens go in for skiing in a big way. Kari skis downhill, using the most up-to-date equipment and the most fashionable attire, Katariina skis cross-country in the traditional way with traditional clothing, and Kalle does incredible tricks and maneuvers on his snowboard wearing the coolest outfit he can get away with.

One of the Kivinens' great pleasures is going to their cottage during the holidays and on warm weekends. The wooden home-away-from-home overlooks a crystal-clear lake and is surrounded by unspoiled forest. They spend lots of quality time together there eating, swimming, discussing, and arranging, but each has their own special interest. Kalle swims, fishes, and bug-watches with a passion. To him this is pure paradise. Wouldn't it be fantastic living in the countryside, he wonders. But he realizes that he'd miss the movies, the computer game arcades, and the youth center too much.

Katariina picks berries, wild flowers, and mushrooms when in season. She adores puttering around her garden where she grows a variety of vegetables. What a terrific existence one would have in the countryside, she ponders. I could survive by writing articles for magazines about country living. But she comprehends that her facts and numbers at work are too important to her to leave behind for very long.

Kari treasures wandering alone through the forest with his camera. He only feels truly relaxed when he is encircled by high trees, wild plants and chirping birds. The fresh scents of the wilderness bring him back to simpler times. He temporarily forgets about deadlines, overtime, taxes, bank loans, and traffic jams. I could make a living here as a nature photographer, he contemplates. But how could I manage without the fine restaurants and rich culture of the city, or without the excitement of planning marketing strategies? Rural life will have to wait for the Kivinen Family.

Reflections on the Seasons

Thoughts on winter

I remember my first winter in Finland well. Especially when it really got cold. I walked outside of my apartment building and the chilly air hit me like a hammer. I could feel the hairs in my nose freezing. I tried to keep my face muscles moving to prevent my cheeks from going numb, and attempted to breathe slowly to avoid frostbitten lungs.

❖ Slippery sidewalks can lead to humiliating falls and a sore bottom. Children and some adults have learned to avoid these problems by using a skating or sliding motion while ambling along. Little granite stones are spread out along the walkways, which definitely help the situation. Unless you get a stone inside your shoe, and then – OUCH – it's misery until you can get to a warm place to take it out.

❖ Sitting out in the snow on a clear, sunny day can be as pleasant as spending a day at the beach, minus the bikinis.

❖ Overall, winter is an excellent time to be in Finland. Because you are a foreigner, Finns will be concerned how you are coping with the cold and may invite you for a hot beverage or a sauna. There are lots of get-togethers during this season, and that makes it convenient to get business or social contacts.

Thoughts on spring

One of the first things you notice about spring is that the days keep getting longer, warmer and brighter. This causes people to start shedding as many winter clothes as possible. Sometimes too soon, and that is probably why there are so many colds during this season.

❖ In early spring, you may see sun-hungry Finns going through a strange ceremony. Whenever the sun breaks through the clouds, they will stop, tilt their heads back, close their eyes and smile; until the sun disappears again and they are off on their way once more.

❖ Uh Oh! It's time to get back in shape. You can't hide under those layers of clothes anymore. Reducing that protruding stomach and those flabby thighs becomes a priority. Men and women go out jogging, visit the local gyms and try out new diets. They are hoping to squeeze into last year's bathing suit.

❖ As the temperature rises and the snow starts melting, streets and sidewalks become a slushy mess. You have to shine your shoes constantly and wash light-color clothing often. And then you are standing on a street corner and suddenly... WATCH OUT! Too late! That car just splashed half melted snow and street dirt all over you.

❖ Just when you believe all of the snow has disappeared and you are ready to say goodbye to the cold season, winter strikes back (*takatalvi* in Finnish). This may happen several times... in the same day.

❖ This is the time you notice the appearance of pretty girls (or handsome men). Everywhere you look! Where were they hiding all winter? The mating season begins.

❖ When the weather is beautiful people become energetic and excited. They sometimes have difficulty concentrating on work. They would rather be outside. If you have any business negotiations or a presentation to make on a nice day, try to be brief and to the point. Or, let the sun work in your favor and suggest to your colleagues that you continue discussions at an outdoor café.

Thoughts on summer

During summer, it seems as if Finns are moving around at double speed, talking vigorously, smiling excessively and generally looking like they just returned from a seminar on "positive thinking." Don't worry this condition is temporary and will soon pass, as soon as the autumn begins.

♣ Summer means bright days, white nights and outdoor barbeques. Thriving plants, colorful flowers, and chirping birds. Sparkling seas, glimmering lakes, and beach parties. It also means hoards of tourists in the cities and hoards of mosquitoes in the countryside.

♣ This is a time to sample freshly picked strawberries, munch on sweet peas straight from the pod, devour sausage right from the grill and savor fish warm from the smoker.

♣ The sea and lakes warm up enough to accommodate hours of pleasant bathing and swimming. And no sharks, stinging jellyfish or crocodiles to worry about – at least I hope not.

✤ In July Finns desert the cities like desperate refugees, so this may not be the best time to come to Finland on business. However, it's a fine time to spend your holidays here.

✤ Remember that summers aren't always like they are portrayed in tourist brochures. It can rain for days at a time or it can be miserably hot (but not very often). So bring a variety of clothes and be ready for anything.

Thoughts on autumn

In early autumn the leaves turn spectacular colors, there are beautiful sunsets (when it's not raining) and the air becomes fresh and crisp.

✤ Cities come alive again and the business atmosphere returns to normal. Finns become motivated and start ambitious projects, study in the evenings and get involved with their hobbies.

✤ This is the time for berry picking, mushroom gathering and hunting.

✤ As the days get shorter and colder, people disappear under layers of clothing and umbrellas. Finns seem to eat more during the autumn (probably because a few extra kilos won't be noticed). Many like to spend time inside cozy cafés sipping a cappuccino, reading a magazine or chatting with friends.

✤ During autumn's gloom the cultural atmosphere blossoms. Museums have special exhibitions, theaters have premier performances and operas are often sold out. Classical, rock and jazz music concerts are everywhere; and for those who love nightlife, there is plenty of it to go around.

♣ This is the time when people are most open to new ideas. It is the season of endless possibilities and opportunities. A great time to do business in Finland!

The Pleasures of Steam

Sauna is the one Finnish word that has really become universal. Though Finns didn't invent the sauna, they have certainly turned out to be the world's undisputed connoisseurs of this pursuit. The sauna is an important part of the Finnish way of life and a symbol of the national culture. There are seminars, health studies and magazines devoted to the benefits and pleasures of this endeavor. Organizations such as the Finnish Sauna Society are highly respected. And, the sauna has its own name day, on the second Saturday of June.

An old Finnish proverb emphasizes its significance asserting, "First build the sauna and then the house." Not only was the sauna used for washing and keeping clean, it was also a hygienic place to give birth, perform folk medicine and smoke meats. It was a place where weary farmers and laborers could ease their sore muscles and smooth their worried minds. And for many rural Finns, a Christmas without a family sauna was unimaginable.

The modern Sauna is a wooden room with benches and a special stove (called *kiuas*). It is usually warmed up to somewhere between 70–110 degrees Celsius. First you take a shower and enter the hot room naked (although in mixed saunas bathing suits may be worn). Then you sit on a wooden bench and throw water onto a pile of stones on top of the stove. This produces steam (called *löyly*), which scalds your skin, makes you sweat and increases your blood circulation. You may be offered a leafy birch whisk called *vihta* or *vasta,* with which Finns gently beat themselves. Don't worry, this process is more pleasant than it sounds. It simply enhances the cleansing effect by opening up the pores, and it gives the body a fresh aroma.

Although most urban saunas are heated by electricity, traditional saunas in the countryside burn wood, which produces a softer, more soothing warmth. The most

esteemed of all is the chimneyless smoke sauna. To prepare a smoke sauna bath one must let the wood burn down until only glowing embers remain. Then the door is closed and the room is allowed to gradually heat up to the right temperature. This is a lengthy process, but true enthusiasts are happy to take the trouble and time in order to partake of a genuine smoke sauna.

It is believed that taking a sauna has many health benefits; at least that's what Finns will persistently tell you. There is another old Finnish proverb that goes, "If sauna, liquor and tar don't help, your condition is fatal." As a matter of fact, medical studies have found the sauna to promote well-being by relaxing muscles, reducing stress and lowering blood pressure. Nonetheless, if you have a serious medical condition, you might want to check with your doctor before diving into a hot sauna.

Some sound advice is to stay in the sauna only as long as you are enjoying it. No need for you to feel like a boiled potato trying to keep up with any macho *steamheads* who insist on having a sizzling marathon. When you've had enough *löyly*, go out and cool off. In summer you might have the opportunity to take a refreshing dip in a lake. In winter, there is sometimes an option for a quick plunge through a hole cut in the ice (called *avanto*), or a stimulating roll in the snow. Then again, you can always decline these chilly suggestions and just take a shower. After that, if you have the will and fortitude, by all means, go back into the heat.

During your stay in this country you'll discover that the sauna is something that unites all Finns. It is for everyone.

Businesspeople use saunas to help with difficult negotiations, politicians meet in saunas to talk over important problems, artists go to the sauna to get inspiration, overstressed workers use the sauna as relaxation medicine, and for some people the sauna is a place to socialize. There is one thing that the sauna is NOT: a place for sex. On the other hand, it is often said that a woman looks most beautiful after a sauna.

Anyway, you'll probably have plenty of occasions to experience a sauna and find out what all the fuss is about. After all, Finland has about 1.7 million saunas, or about one for every three inhabitants. They are located in private houses, apartment buildings, companies, government offices, public swimming pools, bathhouses and summer cottages. Remember, Finns think of the sauna as a necessity, not a luxury.

Alone in the Sauna

I'm tense, I'm stressed
  I've seen the 8:30 news
Thank God it's that time of the week
To visit that delightful place
That temple of warmth and steam
Where a roaring fire transfers its precious heat
To those sacred rocks on the stove
I wash in a shower with attitude
Changing from ice cold to scalding hot at will
Then as I enter the sauna room
Stunning heat strikes me
I dip a cracked ladle into an ancient bucket
Toss out a scoop of water
A direct hit onto the rocks
Stream rises with a harsh hiss
Spreads through the room
It crawls over me and makes me recoil
I take refuge
Dropping my head into my arms
Until the searing and painful fallout passes
I let out an involuntary *"Ahh"*
Many thoughts race through my head
As time passes my mind slows down
Worries evaporate
I recall pleasant memories from the past
My muscles relax

I ponder my present blessings
The future looks brighter
Then after some quiet moments
After some serious sweating
After meditating on pine knots
And sap patterns on the wall
After letting myself drift into nothingness
With only the sound of wood crackling
To enter my thoughts
Answers appear
Maybe from the same inspirations
That Sibelius, Gallen-Kallela and Mannerheim once had
I find enlightenment within my being
That could change the direction of my life
That could leave an impression on the world
More water, more steam, more drifting
Until it is time to get some fresh air
Sit on my towel
Glowing, refreshed, renewed
I leave the sauna and return
To the realities of life
Television droning, kids whining, wife complaining
Bills to be paid, things to be fixed, chores to be done
Now where have those noble expectations gone?
That big Eureka!
That flood of positive energy!
It's here somewhere
Safely inside me
Just waiting
For the next sauna.

Chowtime In Finland

The traditional Finnish diet was influenced by both the east and the west (and in the case of something called *viili*, the influence must have come from outer space). This fare consisted of heavy dishes, meant for the farmer who toiled vigorously in the fields, the laborer who worked long hours with his hands, the housewife who maintained the home with only the most basic of tools… or, anybody who needed enough calories to avoid freezing their backside off in winter (heating and insulation were luxuries in those days).

Availability of ingredients was the most important factor in what people ultimately ate. During wars, economic downturns or famines they might be lucky to get something more than tree bark. In secure times, though, they preferred stews containing lots of meat, root vegetables, fat and plenty of salt. They made dark rye bread or prepared a hard bread that could last long enough to have a first name. They smoked ham and fish in the sauna to preserve them and enhance the flavor. And if fermented drinks with alcohol were available, well, so much the better.

Nowadays, even though very few people do hard manual labor in their jobs anymore, traditional foods are still very popular. One example is *Karelian stew*, made with pork, beef, liver, potatoes, and carrots. *Pyttipannu* is another example of something that will stick to your ribs. It is a hash of ham, potatoes, egg and anything else that is lying around the kitchen. Then everything is fried in butter. Other dishes of this type include meatballs with brown gravy, fried pork doused in thick sauce, and ring sausage filled with cheese.

Health concerns are causing Finns to modify their eating habits. They are trying to reduce fats and salt, decrease portions and add fruits and vegetables to balance out meals. Overeating is usually saved for special occasions, although it's funny how many special occasions there are in this country.

Because you are never far from water in Finland, supper platters are swimming with fish. A local catch, Baltic herring, is eaten in massive quantities. It can be served raw, salted, smoked, charred, fried or prepared in other creative ways such as marinated in lemon or rowanberry sauce. Helsinki hosts the Baltic Herring Market every October.

Fishermen from the Gulf of Finland, the Gulf of Bothnia, and the Åland archipelago sell their bounty from picturesque wooden boats. This flavorsome event is hugely popular.

Salmon and trout are highly prized by the population and served baked, fried, smoked or lightly salted. The recipe for a rich, savory salmon soup is the pride of many households and restaurants. My personal favorite salmon dish consists of cold smoked slices piled on black bread with light mayonnaise and a piece of lettuce or two. Other tasty fish are flounder, perch, pike, cod, pikeperch, and vendace. And not to be missed is *loimusiika* (flamed whitefish). They nail whitefish filets to a board and slowly smoke them over an open flame. The juicy, delightful flavor of this gourmet *oeuvre* will linger in your memory forever.

Everyone knows about Russian caviar, but Finland has its own version. The roe of whitefish, burbot and vendace are extremely delectable and well appreciated by locals and visitors alike. Eat them with sour cream, onions and good bread. Other water-born delicacies include grilled lamprey, smoked eel and in late summer, crayfish (in spite of the way they look, these things ARE edible).

Perhaps what Finns living abroad miss most is the wheel-shaped, rye loaf with the customary hole in the middle. You can't find this kind of bread anywhere else. It has a mild, sour tang and tastes delicious straight from the oven, or it can be stored on a horizontal pole under the ceiling (makes an artistic decoration) until ready for consumption.

Finns love their bread and take pride in the dozens of varieties available: rye, wheat, oat, potato and mixed grain; heavy, light, crisp and unleavened; sour-sweet and malted. Speaking of bread, Finns are among the world's most proficient sandwich architects and aficionados. You may be surprised to see what combinations of ingredients are loaded onto an open face, double or triple-decker sandwich.

The most familiar meats garnishing dinner plates around Finland are pork, chicken and beef. These days it has become more common to encounter turkey, lamb, and duck, too. Some farms have started raising more exotic commodities such as ostriches, wild boar, and snails, but it may be a while before these become mainstream items.

During your stay in Finland you wouldn't want to miss sampling reindeer, that versatile Lapland specialty. You'll find it served in restaurants throughout the country. In better places you will also be able to savor elk, snow grouse, willow grouse, wild duck, pheasant and hare.

Some say Helsinki has the best Russian restaurants outside of St. Petersburg. You may want to try out such dishes as black caviar, salted cucumber with honey and sour cream, borscht soup, *blinis* with mushroom salad, chicken Kiev, spicy beef steak, lamb chops marinated in garlic, or even roast bear.

The sausage is in its own category in Finland. Everybody jokes about the ring sausage (*lenkkimakkara*) and grill sausage (*grillimakkara*), calling them "Finnish vegetables." Yet, every year, Finns consume them in staggering quantities in homes, at festivals, in the woods, and after saunas. The Finnish sausage has come along way, though, and at most butcher shops and markets, next to the traditional favorites, you'll find an assortment of top quality sausage creations.

For those who are not able to indulge in sausages, or partake of any other meats, there is hope. Not long ago, vegetarians had to search relentlessly get an appealing meal. This is no longer the case. Splendid vegetarian restaurants and health food cafés are springing up all the time. Tofu and spouts are here to stay.

Finns are eager consumers of dairy products. Milk and *piimä* (buttermilk) are customary beverages to have with any meal. The yogurt section brims with distinctive Finnish flavors such as *lingonberry*-vanilla or cloudberry. Finnish *emmental*, *edam*, blue and cream cheese have gained international recognition. You may also want to try other Finnish dairy cultures and concoctions, but before you put something called *viili* (fermented milk) into your mouth, be warned – it's not for the fainthearted.

For a unique dessert, try cloudberries and arctic brambleberries, which make a luscious tart or can perk up ice cream. A serving of cheese bread, rhubarb pie or forest blueberry cake will also give you classic Finnish zest. Nevertheless, the king of desserts is that ubiquitous pastry called *pulla*, served day and night. And, you may be wondering about those little

black candies you see Finns so eagerly devouring. They are called *salmiakki*, licorice spiced with ammonium chloride. It takes an acquired taste to appreciate the strong, salty flavor, but try some anyhow. You might like the assault to your taste buds.

Of course, what's a dessert without coffee… or, for that matter, a morning… or, an afternoon… or, an evening. Finns are the #1 coffee drinkers in the world, and usually prefer it very strong. The most prevalent type is simply brewed and filtered, but Finns have happily accepted espressos, cappuccinos, lattes and, unsurprisingly, Irish coffees.

Before leaving this country, you must undergo one of the great culinary experiences, the Finnish Smorgasbord. This is not just a salad bar or a light buffet, but a table straining with so many dishes that you'll feel bewildered just looking at them all. You'll end up sampling so many entrées and treats that you'll waddle away after the meal in a semi-coma.

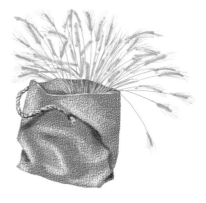

*A few more Finnish
specialties and delicacies:*

Kalakukko – a fish pie
made with layers of
vendace and fatty pork,
backed in a loaf-shaped
pastry.

Korvasienimuhennos – creamed
morel mushroom stew.

Maksalaatikko – liver casserole.

Mustamakkara – blood sausage, a delicacy eaten with
lingonberry sauce.

Hernekeitto – pea soup, usually served on Thursdays with
pancakes.

Karjalanpiirakka – Karelian pasties, a moccasin-shaped,
rye shell filled with rice pudding. Egg butter is often added
to augment the flavor.

Poronkäristys – sautéed reindeer, a special treat in the
south of Finland, an everyday meal in Lapland.

Kaalikääryle – a cabbage roll, it's very easy to eat too many of these scrumptious things.

Lihakeitto – meat soup, a hearty concoction guaranteed to warm and fill you up.

Hirvipaisti – roast elk, a succulent treat during the hunting season.

Uudet perunat – new potatoes, these little delicacies appear in early summer and are anxiously awaited by the whole population.

Kaurapuuro – oatmeal, the Finnish way of beginning the morning.

Tyrnimarjamehu – sea buckthorn juice, naturally tangy and full of vitamins.

Lihapiirakka kahdella nakilla ja kaikilla mausteilla – a meat pie with two hot dogs and all condiments, not a very high quality food but very popular among revelers who have spent a night out on the town and need something to steady their walk. Available at fast-food kiosks in the wee hours of the morning.

Eating on the Town

The place seemed pleasant enough, and I was looking forward to an enjoyable dinner. I glanced up from the menu to see a grim-faced waitress, whom I'll call grumpy, standing by our table. By the sour look on her mug, you'd think she was suffering from constipation. Pekka, a friend who brought me to this well-known restaurant, had recommend pizza. I ordered a *frutti di mare*. Grumpy took our orders and left without comment or changing her expression.

After what seemed like an eternity, our pizzas arrived. I was famished and getting ready to chomp down on the first slice when I noticed something disturbing: Three sharp pieces of mussel shell were staring at me. They certainly wouldn't have done my teeth, stomach or intestines any good.

I was appalled and expected an apology, a new pizza, a complimentary bottle of champagne and, of course, no charge. When I showed Grumpy the pieces of shell, she just shrugged her shoulders, reluctantly changed the pizza for something else, and offered me free coffee for my inconvenience. Then she had the nerve to charge me full price on the bill.

I was angry. Ready to complain to the manager, and tell my story to the newspaper, but Pekka didn't want me to make a fuss. He asked me to keep silent about the matter. "We may want to come here again," he said.

This was my first impression of a Finnish restaurant. Fortunately I visited another place the following week, which was completely different. The waiter was friendly and efficient. He looked like he really enjoyed his work. The food was terrific, too. What a change!

Overall though, during my first years in Finland, high quality restaurants were in short supply and good service was in even shorter supply. True, you could find some gems with delicious and imaginative cuisine, and you could also encounter cheerful and efficient waiters. But more often you stumbled upon eateries that had mediocre cooking and a dour wait staff.

Gradually the second-rate eating-places started fading away in Finland (although you can still find some). New innovative and cordial restaurants of both Finnish and international styles began taking their places. Waiters and waitress shed the old, dull uniforms and began sporting smarter attire. They also began smiling, socializing, and became more sensitive to their customers' needs. True competition had arrived. Owners and chefs discovered how to make their restaurants attractive to clientele by offering better food, a unique theme and a distinctive atmosphere. Today, eating out in Finland is as agreeable an experience as it is in other European countries (often more so)… unless you happen to encounter Grumpy.

Playing Politics

Party symbols surrounding the Parliament Building.

After being ruled for centuries by two powerful neighbors, Finland finally achieved independence in 1917. In 1919 it became a republic, after passing the Constitutional Act. During the following years, clouds of communism, fascism and imperialism circled overhead, but Finland managed to keep its sovereignty and remained a strong democracy.

Finland's Constitution guarantees legal equality, freedom of expression, freedom of religion and conscience, freedom of assembly, freedom to choose one's residence, freedom of movement, and freedom to complain about the weather.

The Finnish people are represented by a 200-member parliament. Members of Parliament are elected to serve a four-year term by direct popular vote. It is the Parliament's duty to pass legislation, approve the national budget, endorse tariffs and treaties with other countries, trade insults with members of other parties, and pretend that they actually accomplished something useful on election year. Anyone with the right to vote may stand for parliament, and as a result you sometimes get some real flaky characters who are, of course, loved by the popular press.

Plenary sessions are chaired by a speaker or deputy speaker – usually someone who can act interested in what members are saying while secretly writing a novel or planning a vacation. These sessions are open to the public, and if you have trouble sleeping, this is a good opportunity to catch up on a few winks.

The President is elected in a separate ballot for a six-year term. This office used to have substantial power, but recently it has been reduced to more of a figurehead role – albeit a powerful figurehead. Nevertheless, the president still has a great deal of influence on foreign policy, appoints the prime minister elected by the parliament, and gets to wear fancy ribbons and metals. Not to mention that she lives in a beautiful mansion, travels in style and has the power to throw some spectacular balls.

The Government, or Council of State, drafts bills and sees that parliamentary decisions are enforced. Since no party ever gets a clear majority, the government must be formed by coalition. In other words, parties who have been calling other parties malicious names and blaming them for everything that's gone wrong in the last decade, including bad weather, suddenly have to do a complete aboutface and say, "Of course we can work closely together with those fine people, we have so much in common..."

Within the government, there are 13 different ministries with 17 ministers, plus the Prime Minister who heads the team. They could probably cut this number down a bit, but with all the parties in the governing coalition, you've got to let everyone feel important.

There are three main political parties that have long been the major power players: the Social Democrats (left of the right but right of the left), the Center Party (we are either rural urbanites or urban rednecks), and Conservatives (the country needs reform, but we don't want to offend anybody). Other significant parties include: the Greens – (ecology and conservation can be trendy), the League of the Left (what's wrong with high taxes?), the Swedish People's Party (we'll form a government with anyone), and the Christian Democrats (no fun without guilt).

The judicial branch of government is independent of the other branches – although the president appoints the judges in the first place. There are three levels of courts in civil and criminal cases: the general courts, the Court of Appeal, and the Supreme Court. Cases are decided by magistrates and judges rather than by juries. Therefore cases tend to move more efficiently than under the British or American systems. Lawyers deliver a less emotional and more factual appeal. And, unfortunately for law firms, lawsuit awards are generally kept to realistic levels.

Good in Sports and Good Sports

Finland is a country of sports devotees. Some of the population go out at every possible opportunity, sweating, straining, huffing and puffing; while others sit on sofas watching every possible sports competition on television eating greasy, sugary food and washing it down with beer. Most Finns, however, are somewhere in-between these extremes.

This is a nation of loyal fans and there are plenty of heroes to cheer. Finnish athletes have had an admirable number of winners in the Olympics and in other world championships, but anytime a Finn wins an event, no matter how obscure, he is considered a national hero.

Whether you are a participant or a spectator, sport is almost always a welcome subject to break the ice at business or social gatherings, or to cool things down when negotiations get tough.

A Brief Glimpse of Finland's Champs

Finland has a long history in athletics. The man who is credited with "running Finland onto the world map" is Hannes Kolehmainen when he won the 5,000-meter race, the 10,000-meter race and the marathon in 1912 at the Stockholm Olympics. Paavo Nurmi was called the "Flying Finn" because of his domination of running events between 1920 and 1928. He won nine gold and three silver Olympic medals. At about the same time period, Ville Ritola won five gold medals. More recently Lasse Virén won the 5,000 and 10,000-meter events in the 1972 and 1976 Olympics. Lately, Finland has done well in distance walking, shot put and javelin. Nevertheless, whether Finns are winning or not, track and field is highly admired in this country and you'll

Paavo Nurmi

find that Finnish enthusiasts are extremely knowledgeable about the sport.

Finns have always excelled on skis, and have consistently taken home medals in Nordic skiing events. One of the all time legends is Marja-Liisa Kirvesniemi who continued winning at an age when most competitors had long retired. A new hero, Samppa Lajunen, made his name at the 2002 winter Olympics by grabbing 3 gold medals in the Nordic Combined. The Finnish ski jump team has, for a long time, been a force to reckon with, and nobody will ever forget the unbeatable Matti Nykänen who won as many medals as he has had marriages. In the past, Finland hasn't been a strong contender in slalom. However, Kalle Palander won the first world championship in 1999.

No sport can spark passionate feelings like ice hockey.

Matti Nykänen

The Finnish team is consistently one of the world's finest. Finland has been a significant supplier of players to the NHL, including Teemu Selänne who is called the Finnish Flash.

Driving around relentlessly seems to be a Finnish instinct (just look at some of the drivers on the Finnish roads). Keke Rosberg and Mika Häkkinen both won world championships in Formula One racing. Tommy Mäkinen, Juha Kankkunen and Ari Vatanen have all won world championships in Rally Driving.

Jari Litmanen, Finland's best soccer star, is currently playing for Barcelona. Jani Sievinen demonstrated to the world what a Finn can achieve in a swimming pool. Petri Kokko and Susanna Rahkamo who won a gold medal in the European championships in ice dancing are still practicing their art as professionals.

Finland also does well in wrestling, motorcycle racing, curling, orienteering and rowing. They have respectable soccer, handball, basketball and volleyball teams. Finland even has several American football teams who can hold their own with their European rivals.

You'll find plenty of spectator events to observe in this country, including trotting races, floor ball games or even ice pool competitions. If you would like to encounter a sport that is exceedingly Finnish, go take in a *pesäpallo* game. It was adapted from American baseball by Lauri Pihkala to suit the Finnish approach to sport. It is extremely popular, even small towns have first-rate teams. At first it might seem like a peculiar sport with indistinguishable rules, but after watching the game together with Finns for a while, you can't help but get caught up in their enthusiasm.

Getting in Motion During Summer

Walking – This is the most popular activity in Finland. Cities and towns are pedestrian friendly and generously interspersed with walking paths, pedestrian streets and parks. Walking is the best way of seeing the sights, giving you plenty of time to absorb the wealth of attractions.

Nordic walking – The technique of using specially designed poles to intensify exercise. It is 40 to 50% more efficient than walking without poles. It develops arms, shoulders and chest muscles while building up endurance in the legs. Nordic walking does not aggravate joints and knees. Over 1,000,000 Finns have tried this activity. Why not give it a go?

Hiking – The majority of the Finnish landscape is forested, so there is no shortage of places to trek in solitude.

Maps are available for every section in the country. The most uncomplicated way to take an outing is to follow one of the many marked trails. For a longer excursion, consider hiring a guide.

Cycling – Cycling is a cheap, convenient way of getting around cities and towns. Cycling out in the countryside is a fantastic way to view the picturesque landscape and rustic villages. Bikes can be hired at almost every locality and there are plenty of back roads on which to use them. Get a mountain bike and you will have an unlimited number of trails to explore in the woods.

Canoeing, rowing, kayaking – enjoy the beautiful, unspoiled environment while propelling yourself at your own pace. Feel the splash of cool water, inhale fresh air and enjoy the scenery from an exceptional point of view.

Swimming – With all the clean water in the lakes and sea you can always find a beach of your own, or if you like company, pick one of the popular public ones. There are no sharks or crocodiles. Though, once in a while someone gets a nip from a disgruntled pike.

Golf – Although the season is short, it is intense with so many hours of sunlight during the summer. The well-kept, un-crowded and beautiful courses make it a real joy to play this sport, even if you don't play very well.

There are many other sports you can do during the summer such as river rafting, water-skiing and rock climbing, to name but a few. Best to contact the local tourist office for the names of organizers who rent out equipment and arrange outings. But, if you don't feel very energetic, then just indulge in that activity so well loved by Finns: sun bathing.

Winter Workout

Cross-country skiing – Finland has a long tradition of cross-country skiing. Sometimes described as the perfect sport, it exercises virtually every muscle in the body. In winter you can ski just about anywhere. No lift tickets to buy, no waiting in lines, just get moving and admire Finland's beautiful winter landscapes.

Downhill skiing – Finland has plenty of snow for downhill skiing although there are no high mountains. Ski resorts are located all over Finland, but the best ones are found in the eastern and northern parts of the county.

Sledding – One of the most basic forms of winter activity is to simply take a sled, walk up to the nearest hill and plunge down. Your sled can be anything from a plastic disc to a fancy racing model. Watch out for trees, rocks, roads and other people before getting in motion.

Ice skating – Outdoor rinks are everywhere and skate rentals are available at some of them. Wear protective clothing, use good gloves and watch out for wild hockey players.

Kick sledding – This is an old Finnish means of transportation for getting around on lakes, icy country roads and snowy forest trails. With the new innovative models, it makes for a fun yet uncomplicated sport.

Snowshoe walking – This activity has been around for a long time, but with new materials and techniques, moving across heavy snow has gotten much easier.

Snowmobiling, dog sledding and reindeer sleigh riding are enjoyable activities that are best tried at one of the many winter resorts around Finland.

Go indoors – When the cold gets too much for you, simply change to an indoor activity. There are gyms and swimming pools, and in larger towns you can find indoor golf courses, bowling alleys, roller blade rinks and billiard rooms.

What if you get a sprain, strain or pain while participating in a sport activity? No problem. Finland has an abundance of physiotherapists, masseurs and doctors, or you can try the Finnish therapy method of sauna and beer.

Ukko, the supreme god

Keeping the Faith

The ancient Finns had their own indigenous religious traditions. Their gods included *Ilmarinen*, god of weather; *Ahti*, god of water and fish; *Tapio*, god of forests; *Ukko*, the supreme god and, of course, his wife *Rauni* who might have been goddess of shopping. Ancient businessmen probably wanted to get on the good side of *Kratti*, guardian of wealth, and housewives needed to take care of *Tonttu*, guardian of the home. My personal favorite is *Kekri*, who apparently was the god of celebrating. But everybody had to watch out for *Piru*, though, because he was quite a devil.

Around the 12th century Sweden came over and brought Catholicism with them. This turned out to be a pretty popular religion, although there were a few disgruntled pagans. A prominent example was a fellow called *Lalli* who killed St. Henry, the first bishop. By the 14th century, most of Finland was under Catholic domination and Swedish rule. This lasted a few hundred years until the Swedish king decided to embrace the Protestant Reformation. He liked the doctrines of the new church, especially the idea of reducing the secular power of the church and transferring its income and property to the crown. So the Finns gradually converted to Lutheranism, which became the official state religion. The vast majority of the population (85%) still belongs to the Lutheran church today.

Orthodox Christianity is the other official religion. It was brought over when Finland became a Grand Duchy of the Russian Empire. Just over 1% of the population belongs to the Orthodox Church. Other Christian denominations represented in Finland include Pentecostals, Jehovah's Witnesses, the Free Church, Seventh Day Adventists, Mormons, Roman Catholics, Methodists and Baptists.

Judaism came to Finland in the 19th century through Jewish merchants and men working for the imperial army. There are presently 1,200 Jews living in Finland, mainly in Helsinki and Turku. Muslims first came to Finland with the Russian army toward the end of the 19th century. The Islamic community remained small until recently when immigration increased their numbers significantly. Nowadays, just about every major world religion is represented in Finland.

The church plays an important role in baptisms, marriages, funerals and confirmations (over 90% of Finnish youth attend a confirmation camp). It collects taxes and registers births. By employing its own social, youth and day care workers, the church gets involved in the community. They help the aged, the disabled, alcoholics and drug addicts; and counseling is given to families with social and financial problems.

Most Finns do not think of themselves as very religious, but want to belong to an organized church. They don't go regularly to church but attend a service several times during the year, especially on important holidays. The majority of Finns are believers, and many have their own personal ways of being reverent. They would like to maintain good relations with the higher powers. After all, if there is an afterlife, they hope to end up in a place as divine as Finland.

finns with Pens

Until the 19th century, most Finnish literature was written in Swedish or Latin. Finnish language folklore and heritage was preserved in oral myths, songs and poems. Thereafter, Finnish writers began a productive period of rich literature in both Swedish and Finnish.

J.L. Runeberg (1804–77) wrote patriotic ballads, composed the lyrics of Finland's national anthem and became known as the national poet. Zacharias Topelius (1818–98) wrote creative fairy tales. Aleksis Kivi (1834–72) is credited with being the founder of modern Finnish literature. His classic epic, Seven Brothers, has been widely translated.

Mika Waltari

The poetry of Eino Leino (1878–1926) combined folk poetry and symbolism. It exerted great influence on the written word at the beginning of the 20th century. Frans Emil Sillanpää (1888–1964), a novelist and short story writer, was the only Finn to ever win a Nobel Prize for literature. Mika Waltari was famous for his historical novels, of which The Egyptian was made into a Hollywood movie (most people say the book was better).

Today, Finland's writers are producing great numbers of novels, short stories and poems. Many of these have been translated and can be found in the larger bookshops. Perhaps the most commercially successful writer in Finland was Tove Jansson. Her troll characters, Moomin and friends, are known in over 30 languages. You can also see them on videos and computer CDs… not to mention the Moomin World amusement park in the town of Naantali. Moonin must be the world's richest troll.

Tove Jansson

Let's Do the Kalevala

For many years, the area in Finland with the richest oral folklore traditions has been in the east. That doesn't surprise me a bit, because the Karelians have always been known as big talkers. However, it was just a matter of time, with all the yellow journalism and cheap novels around, that the stories of yore would be lost forever. Fortunately, a doctor and poet, and perhaps a man who knew a good potential market, did something about it. Elias Lönnrot (1802–84) wandered around remote districts of eastern Finland and collected stories, poems, songs and perhaps shopping lists. From these he created a masterpiece of poetry that has become a national epic. He published his first version in 1835 and another version (the one used today) in 1849.

The stories in the *Kalevala* are about two imaginary countries: P*ohjola* (the bad guys) and *Kalevala* (the good guys). Some of the main characters are: Väinämöinen – a bearded old wisecracker, who sings, is a good raconteur and looks a bit like Moses. Aino – a good-looking blond who commits suicide to avoid marrying Väinämöinen (did he have bad breath or what?). Kullervo – suffers from some kind of curse or maybe he needs to see a psychiatrist. Ilmarinen – created the *Sampo*, which contains mystical powers and can provide anything you need, because they didn't have a Stockmann department store in those days.

The *Kalevala* became an international success and has been translated into over 40 languages. It has been the stimulus for famous Finnish artists and composers. They say it is the foundation of Finnish history, culture and literature. There is even a *Kalevala Day* celebrated on February 28th. Nowadays, every Finnish pupil must learn about the *Kalevala*, but don't ask them for too many details. Everyone seems to have his own vague ideas about what it really says and means. The best thing is to go to a bookstore and get your own copy. Finns would like to hear your opinion of the great epic.

Ilmarinen – created the Sampo, which contains mystical powers and can provide anything you need.

Music in the Air

Even though Finland hasn't won a Eurovision contest yet, I still consider it a very musical country. Music goes back to the roots of Finnish culture and continues to influence, and be influenced by, the society's development.

Traditional Finnish folk music blends elements of both eastern and western cultures. Combinations of violins, clarinets, accordions, kanteles (the national instrument) and singing produce polkas, polonaises, minuets, marches and mazurkas. Some modern folk groups, such as *Värttinä* have achieved great success by bringing together traditional music with rock, jazz and other popular sounds.

Finland has had more than its share of gifted classical music composers. The most famous was Jean Sibelius who, some say, got his inspiration in the sauna. Contemporary

Finnish composers such as Aulis Sallinen and Ilkka Kuusisto continue to gain world fame. Internationally known conductors include such names as Paavo Berglund, Leif Segerstam and Esa-Pekka Salonen. Some of the opera singers who often make the circuit abroad are Matti Salminen, Karita Mattila and Monika Groop. And instrumentalists such as pianist Olli Mustonen are always in demand.

This small country contains a diversity of musicians: melancholy tango singers, *jenkka* crooners, romantic wailers, as well as jazz groups, big bands and experimental orchestras. Finnish Pop and evergreen music include translations from other languages and Finland's own homegrown syrupy sounds with names such as Jari Sillanpää, Eino Grön and Arja Koriseva making the public happy.

Ever since its beginning, rock 'n' roll music has had a great following in Finland. Although there have been many popular groups, the first to achieve international success was probably the Hanoi Rocks in the 1980s. Later the Leningrad Cowboys toured around Europe and even starred in their own film. Today, the best-known Finnish groups whose music has made it abroad are: HIM, a love metal band; Bomfunk Mc's, a hip-hop/funk band; and Nightwish, a rock band with nuances of opera.

So, about the Eurovision contest. If Finland doesn't win, people will tell you that it doesn't matter, because nobody pays attention to that sort of thing anyway. But, if Finland wins, there will be three days of celebration, and maybe a national holiday.

Let's Dance

It's true that Finland has an outstanding selection of dance entertainment, including ballet, modern dance and aerobic dance performances. All the same, Finns love to get up and boogie themselves. There is no shortage of dancing opportunities in Finland. Every city and town has its dance restaurants, where the young and young-at-heart can wear out their shoes until the early hours of the morning. You can easily find places that feature rock´n roll, heavy metal, jazz, techno, soul, funk or hip-hop by either asking around or checking the local newspaper.

For a more traditional atmosphere, you can check out one of the dance restaurants where patrons do the waltz, tango, *humppa*, j*enkka*, and the foxtrot. These restaurants usually feature a small orchestra that plays "old favorites" and "evergreen

Rääkkylän

tunes." They are eager to take any requests, so long as the songs are at least twenty years old, or at least sound that way.

In this kind of dance restaurant, a man should feel free to ask any woman to dance, as it is considered good

manners to say *"yes"* to any male who is not drunk and has taken a shower within the last 48 hours. You normally have two dances and then the gentleman should accompany the lady back to her chair and exchange polite *thank-you's*. Sometimes you see *Naistentanssit* advertised, meaning ladies' choice. If a woman asks a man to dance, he should accept her offer graciously as most of the ladies don't like to be refused. I've even seen women physically dragging reluctant males onto the dance floor. If you don't feel like dancing, sit quietly at the bar.

If you are in Finland during the summer, take the opportunity to visit an outdoor pavilion dance called *lavatanssit*. These charming places are located in what seems to be the middle of nowhere, but these dances attract large numbers of people and the atmosphere is lively.

Folk dance is mainly a spectator sport these days. On the other hand, at certain festivals and parties, everyone is encouraged to do these old-time dances. If you find yourself in a situation where you are asked to participate, don't worry, just hop along with everybody else and act like you know what you are doing – kind of like business negotiations.

Down the Finnish Hatch

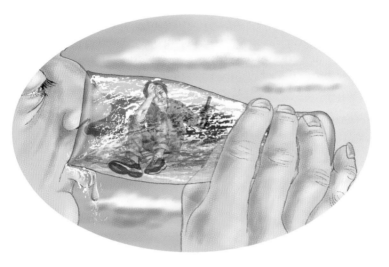

When you see alcoholics overtly staggering around the city streets, or notice teenagers hopelessly intoxicated on the weekend in the local park, it's easy to make quick judgments about the Finnish drinking culture. In fact, Finns may declare, "We can't quit until the bottle is empty," or "We only drink to get drunk."

Actually Finns don't drink as much as it would seem. According to statistics, Finnish yearly alcohol consumption is below the average in Europe. During recent years, Finns have been drinking more wine and less vodka, and taste rather than just alcohol content has become the basis for choosing a beer. But as Finns will admit, this is a not yet a country of liquor connoisseurs.

In contrast to many central and southern European countries, Finland has not always had an open or positive relationship with alcohol. From 1866 to 1968 alcoholic beverages have been highly restricted, and from 1919 to 1932 there was a complete prohibition. Leaders of the temperance movement thought that making spirits illegal would eliminate social and health problems. The effect was quite the opposite. Enterprising smugglers brought in so much illegal booze that it was available day and night to a thirsty population. Lawmakers had to make alcohol legal again so they could get it and crime under control.

The company that was established to restrain liquor consumption was called *Alkoholiliike*, later changed to ALKO. This monopoly soon became a huge company, which for years completely regulated the import, production, distribution and sales of alcoholic beverages. Naturally, it always made a considerable profit, which among other things was used to get people to consume less alcohol. They were advertising against their own product. However, this only enticed people to want to taste the "evils of alcohol" even more. What a business!

Holiday Scenes

Independence Day (*itsenäisyyspäivä*) – A solemn and reflective day to mark Finland's independence from Russia in 1917. This holiday is celebrated with patriotic speeches, visits to cemeteries, parades, concerts and special church services. For this occasion people put blue and white candles on their windowsills, bakeries create blue and white pastries, and shops set up blue and white displays. Finnish flags are everywhere. Many Finns take pleasure at this time in having a festive meal at a restaurant with friends and relatives. There are numerous formal and informal social events throughout the country. Though the highlight comes in the evening when the President holds a huge formal ball at the palace for the *crème de la crème*. Half the population is glued to the TV trying to recognize who is shaking the President's hand, who is wearing that outrageous outfit, and who is dancing with whom.

Christmas (*joulu*) – The festivities begin already in late November. Because these holidays coincide with the darkest period, Finns really look forward to the colored lights, carols and decorations to brighten up the atmosphere. Suddenly goodwill is given out all over the city in the form of mulled wine (*glögi*), prune-filled, star-shaped pastries (*joulutähdet*), and gingerbread cookies (*piparit*). Shops compete with each other to create the most appealing and attention-grabbing display windows.

Then come the Christmas parties (*pikkujoulut*). Lots of them. Instant Christmas cheer, songs and happy dialogue. Some of these may be minor get-togethers while others are major events with lavish food, live entertainment, and exchange of gag-gifts. It is amazingly easy to drink too many glasses of supercharged mulled wine at one of these occasions. Sometimes unsociable people become friendly with colleagues they would normally never utter a word to, shy people entertain others with jokes and stories, or cautious people reveal their secret romantic feelings to an unsuspecting workmate. Of course, all this is forgotten the next day.

Christmas Eve and Christmas Day are mainly family celebrations. Almost everything is closed, and if you are on your own, this is not a good time to be in Finland. However, if you get invited to a family celebration, you'll probably have a Christmas sauna, listen to Christmas music, decorate the Christmas tree with all sorts of curious items and sing a few carols. You'll go out to the cemetery to light candles on relatives' graves and take a leisurely walk in a park. If you happen to be in the countryside you might go sledding, make a snowman or light large wood candles in the snow.

The Christmas dinner is usually a delectable affair. Spread out over the table will be ham (or turkey), salmon, pickled herring, boiled potatoes, carrot, sweet potato and rutabaga casseroles, *rosolli* salad, rice pudding, fruit soup and homemade beer. As always, there will be plenty of heavy-duty coffee and seasonal pastries.

Santa Claus will come over (often a hired student) and frighten the kids, until they notice he has presents for them. They will shyly take their packages, rip them open and in a few hours every toy will be broken or abandoned forever. The religious people will attend mass; the others will watch special holiday programs on TV. Everyone will sneak into the kitchen late at night and nibble on leftovers.

Boxing Day (*tapaninpäivä*) — Celebrated on the 26th of December, the point of this holiday is to go out and visit friends. The family is wonderful, but after two days of hearing the same stories, it's nice to talk to someone else for a while.

New Year's Eve (*uudenvuodenaatto*) – This is the time to stay up late and welcome in the New Year with a bang – literally with brilliant displays of fireworks, and figuratively with plenty of drinking and partying. It's a custom to melt tin in a dipper and pour it into a bucket of cold water. The resulting sculpture is then interpreted and the future is predicted.

Another important aspect of New Year's Eve is making promises that probably won't be kept but sound sincere at the time. And it goes without saying that at the stroke of midnight there will be a lot of kissing and hugging. Late at night, if you are still awake, you will probably want something salty such as a *nakki* (frankfurter) and potato salad.

Epiphany (*loppiainen*) – On January 6th it's time to eat a few goodies, take down the Christmas tree and put away Christmas decorations. At this point you are so tired of Christmas music that you don't want to hear another carol until next year.

Runeberg Day – On February 5th Finns pay tribute to their national poet, Johan Runeberg, who wrote, among other notable works, the national anthem. Finns take time to enjoy a Runeberg tart, a special pastry originally created by the Poet's wife.

Shrove Sunday and Shrove Tuesday (*laskiainen*) – These two days are celebrated six weeks before Easter by sledding down a hill, skiing, or just playing in the snow. Afterwards Finns are eager to relax and have a Shrovetide bun or pea soup.

Kalevala Day – February 28 is the day devoted to the great Finnish epic poem, the *Kalevala*. Dr. Elias Lönnrot collected these legends in Karelia and published them in 1835. This collection has had a major impact on the cultural life of Finland.

Easter (*pääsiäinen*) – The most important religious celebration in Finland. People flock to religious services, passion plays and religious concerts. Popular secular traditions include growing grass on plates indoors (remember, there is no grass outdoors yet), decorating Easter eggs and making Easter cards. On Palm Sunday children dress up as witches, go door-to-door giving out

Mämmi tastes better than it looks.

decorated pussy willow sprigs and reciting a special verse.
In return they are rewarded with candy or money for this
"service."

    Besides eating chocolate Easter eggs, Finns scarf down a
lot of malt pudding called *mämmi*, which tastes better than
it looks, and sometimes a very sweet concoction called
pasha. It is also a tradition to eat roast lamb at this time,
even if you don't particularly care for lamb.

May Day (*vappu*) – An unsuspecting visitor arriving on the last day of April might think there is massive civil unrest in the country. He needn't be concerned. This is only the Finnish way of celebrating the spring (or the coming of summer). Students put on their white student caps and party wildly in the streets, in homes and in restaurants – for that matter, so does the rest of the population. Cities and towns are covered in helium-filled balloons, streamers and empty bottles. Most Finns treat themselves to *sima*, a yeast-fermented, bubbly drink and *tippaleipä*, a delicious pastry that looks like a bunch of worms.

On May 1st, the next day, there are speeches and champagne picnics with people feasting on sausage, herring or pea soup. The International Labor Movement is also commemorated on this day by parades.

The two-day extravaganza uses up a lot of energy and many people have major hangovers, so don't plan any important projects for May 2nd.

Name Day (*nimipäivä*) – Almost everyone has a Name Day in Finland. You can find it in the calendar or an almanac. If you want to make a big hit with a Finn, you should remember their day with a card, flowers, a small gift or an offer of a cup of coffee.

Fun Festivities

Here is a sampling of the 62 festivals belonging to the Finland Festivals organization. For a complete listing and more information, visit their website at www.festivals.fi.

❖ Avanti Summer Sounds
❖ Festival of Workers' Music
❖ Full Moon Dance Festival
❖ Häme Castle Children's Festival
❖ Imatra Big Band Festival
❖ Järvenpää Sibelius Festival
❖ Jyväskylä Arts Festival
❖ Kaustinen Folk Festival
❖ Kotka Maritime Festival
❖ Kuopio Dance Festival
❖ Lakeside Blues Festival
❖ Pori Jazz Festival
❖ Savonlinna Opera Festival
❖ Tampere International Theater Festival
❖ Tango Festival
❖ Vaasa Choir Festival

Other smaller events are organized by communities or organizations. Here are a few of the more unusual ones that reveal the Finnish sense of humor. Contact the Finnish Tourist Board at www.mek.fi for further information.

Wife Carrying World Championships (Sonkajärvi)
Birch Bark Baking Festival (Punkaharju)
Flirting, National Championships (Kurikka)
Chatting Up Contest For Singles (Kuusamo)
Swarming Around A Field Festival (Kangasniemi)
Husband And Wife Calling (Puolanka)
Scarecrow Exhibition (Ristiina)
Sandcastle Building, National Championships (Hailuoto)
Highway Dancing, National Championships (Lammi)
Boot Throw, World Championships (Pielavesi)
Swamp Football, World Championships (Hämeenkoski)
Finger Pulling, World Championships (Tammela)
Kissing Festival (Ruovesi)
Snowmobile Watercross (Inari)
Arguing Competition, National Championships
(Lappeenranta)

The Longest Day

Unlike some of the other Finnish holidays, on Midsummer you don't get the feeling that you "have to" have a good time. There is a much more relaxed atmosphere. It doesn't really matter what you do and where you are, you are just happy to be at the high point of summer, feeling the magic of the moment.

The traditional Midsummer (*juhannus* in Finnish) was celebrated on the 24th of June, but I guess some modern Finns decided the holiday would be more convenient on a Saturday. Hence, it can fall on any date between the 20th and the 26th of June. Midsummer was originally a pagan celebration, but the church has made the holiday more acceptable to the religiously inclined by slipping John the Baptist into the package. And to make patriots happy, it is an official flag day.

In the old days young girls used to lean over wells naked in order to see their future groom's reflection. Even if the naked girl didn't see any reflections, she probably ended up with plenty of potential grooms lurking around the well. Another quaint custom was that women would roll around naked in wet grass to cast some kind of romantic spell. Call me old-fashioned, but I believe this custom should continue — in the name of culture, of course. Women would also gather seven kinds of flowers or put nine herbs under their pillows believing this to be an aphrodisiac. And what did the men do? What they always do in situations of uncertainty: build something. In this case they erected giant Midsummer poles.

These days on Midsummer, half the population waits in huge lines at supermarkets buying a year's worth of supplies, waits in huge lines at gasoline stations paying the year's highest prices and waits in huge traffic jams trying to leave the city so they can relax at their country cottages by repairing all the winter damages. The other half gets married.

My first Midsummer in Finland was spent on an island in the middle of the Turku Archipelago. After overloading

ourselves with sufficient amounts of consumables and alcoholic beverages, my companions and I lay motionless on a pier watching the sky darken, and then watching it lighten again. During these hours of bliss we were probably uttering over-repeated stories, worn-out clichés, and complete nonsense to each other, but at the time we believed we were imparting great philosophical pearls of wisdom. That must have been the magic of Midsummer at work.

Several of my Midsummers have been spent at Seurasaari Island in Helsinki. This was a good place to take my father when he was visiting me. There would always be fortune tellers, wood carvers, freshly-made pancakes, and of

course the vital *makkara* sausage. Ordinary *makkara* becomes much more appetizing when well-burnt over an open fire, or at least on Midsummer it does. Then there was the folk music, the folk dancing, the folk games, and a man telling folk jokes for which I hadn't the slightest clue why everybody was laughing their heads off. The finale would come when they lit an enormous bonfire and a newly married couple cruised around in an old-fashioned boat. Romantic, but if it were me I'd get a little fishing in at the same time.

The *juhannus* I spent in the city of Jyväskylä was a period of great relaxation. So relaxing was it that I hardly remember what I did for three days other than swim in the unusually warm water and go on a "Special Midsummer" cruise. The Special Midsummer meant that they put lots of tree branches all over the boat and played waltzes and tangos. The passengers kept saying *"Hyvää juhannusta"* to each other. It looked like a smiling contest was taking place.

The Midsummer program I once witnessed in the city of Lappeenranta didn't contain anything extraordinary. In fact it was on a much smaller scale than the one at Seurasaari. What made it unique was the attitude of the spectators. When the orchestra played people looked pleased, when the dancers performed people got excited, when the children's choir sang people were delighted, when there was a boat race people became enthusiastic, and when the bonfire was lit people were completely enchanted by the spectacle. I had no choice but to become cheerful myself.

Unquestionably, I've had my share of appealing Midsummers. One time it was spent in a little fishing village in the far north of Norway. Another time I attended a grand celebration on a farm outside Paris sponsored by the Ministry of Agriculture. And I have terrific memories of several summer cottages visited during this holiday. However, my most memorable Midsummers were spent with my old friend, Mikko. Our routine went as follows: Sauna and swimming at his home in Varkaus. An hour's ride in Mikko's little motor boat down Lake Saimaa to Mauri and his wife's country house. Dining on grilled pork chops and new potatoes on a lakeshore surrounded by verdant forests. A boat ride to the nearby village. Entry to a summer restaurant. Dancing until 2:00 in the morning (although normally I'm a terrible dancer, I seem to do much better on Midsummer).

After that we would go to the village square, get a *porilainen* sandwich or a meat pie with everything at one of the kiosks, and talk with the rest of the village in the white night. This would continue until six or seven in the morning. Then we would take a taxi back to Mauri's place for a morning sauna. Often several of the village residents would end up there, too. For lunch we would have smoked salmon, after which, Mikko and I would head back by boat to Varkaus, stopping off at an island or three to sunbathe. Admittedly, there was nothing remarkable in this routine, but it all added up to a wondrous experience. There was definitely magic in the air.

My kind of Town

"Hey, this really *IS* a nice town," visiting friends sometimes tell me. As if they were informing me of something I didn't already know. Helsinki is one of the world's most welcoming capitals, and both business people and tourists generously award it with positive comments. The natural beauty, the cleanliness and the feeling of security impress most visitors. They also appreciate the plentiful cultural activities, the rich nightlife and the efficient public transportation. Most importantly, though, the residents are amiable and friendly.

The sea has always been the lifeline of this city. Harbors, rocky shores, beaches, islands, together with an armada of ships, ferries, yachts and motorboats give Helsinki its maritime ambiance. Complementing the abundance of water are the pristine forests that surround the city and luxuriant parks that decorate the metropolis. In fact, one third of the city is green space.

Helsinki has 540,000 inhabitants, but when you include the suburbs, that figure comes to almost a million. The neighboring cities of Espoo and Vantaa have a rich variety of interesting sights and attractions and each has a its own tourist office. The whole place is referred to as the Greater Helsinki Area, or the Capital Region.

It all started in 1550. King Gustavus of Sweden thought it was a great idea to start a new town at the mouth of the Vantaa River. His subjects didn't share his enthusiasm and

the settlement grew rather slowly. In 1640 Queen Christina provided a woman's touch and moved the town to its present location, which succeeded in bringing in a few more residents. Then in 1748, Sweden started constructing the fortress of Suomenlinna and employment opportunities beckoned skilled workers. Wanted: cannon makers, masons, cobblers and lots of soldiers.

Life was not always easy in the budding town. There were plagues, raids, famines, fires, and a severe lack of fine cafés. The impenetrable Suomenlinna Fortress didn't help much either, because the Russians took over Finland anyway. However, that turned out to be a good thing, because they made Helsinki the new capital in 1812 and set about fixing up the place.

Nowadays after years of steady development, Helsinki has progressed into a modern city with a healthy respect for its past. Many historical sights, cultural venues, shops and restaurants can easily be reached on foot. Getting around by bicycle is also easy thanks to all the bike paths interspersing the city. And for moving around town, the fleet of buses, trams, local trains, waterbuses and the metro are efficient and convenient.

Helsinki's Top Ten Sights:

Senate Square is a neoclassic center created by Johan Albrecht Ehrenström and Carl Ludvig Engel between 1818 and 1852. The most distinctive buildings are the Government Palace, the City Administration, the University, the University library, the Sederholm House (the oldest building in the city) and the impressive Lutheran Cathedral that dominates the square. In the center of the square towers a statue of Czar Alexander II who will be happy to pose for a photo with you.

The Market Square is a picturesque, lively, outdoor market bordered by a harbor and interesting buildings (well, most buildings are interesting, anyway). Eye-pleasing displays of fruit, vegetables, fish, handicrafts and some rather unusual souvenirs are here for your inspection. You may want to try "the best meat pie in Finland," or, if you are a vegetarian, a *Karelian* pasty. In summer you can purchase sweet peas, strawberries or smoked fish, and devour them alfresco.

The Sibelius Monument was created in 1967 by Eila Hiltunen in honor of Finland's most famous composer, Jean Sibelius. Hundreds of steel pipes were welded together to form this majestic structure located in a serene park setting. It is especially dazzling when viewed from up close.

Suomenlinna is considered to be one of the world's unique treasures by UNESCO. This historical monument, built on six islands, is the largest historical sea fortress in Scandinavia. There are 200 buildings on Suomenlinna, most dating back to the 18th century. Take walks around the fortified walls, visit the museums and art galleries, enjoy the vista points overlooking the sea, have a picnic, or relax in one of the restaurants.

Seurasaari Island is a thickly wooded national park where you can feed squirrels, watch Canadian geese and listen to the hammering of woodpeckers. Following the well-maintained walking paths, you will come to an open-air museum featuring old houses, barns, and granaries from all over Finland. There are beaches, picnic areas and festival grounds. The old church there is a very popular place for summer weddings.

Töölö Bay is a sheltered sea bay in the center of the city. On the eastern rocky outcrops you enjoy exceptional views of the city: Finlandia Hall, the Opera House, the Stadium Tower, the National Museum Tower, and the Central Park. From the other side you gaze at the rustic old villas of Linnunlaulu built in the 1880s. At night, a walk along this 2.2-kilometer path is spectacular.

The Stadium Tower is a well-situated 72-meter structure where you get a bird's-eye view of the city. Take the lift to the top and spend as much time as you like enjoying the sights, the greenery and the sea from this dizzying height.

Kaivopuisto is an attractive green space encircled by wealthy residences, embassies, old villas and water. The park has comfortable lawns, large trees, lively cafés, a small observatory and inviting walking paths. From the gentle hills you appreciate delightful views of the sea, boats, and the archipelago. For a bit of cultural enlightenment, observe the locals as they diligently wash their multihued rugs in the sea.

Temppeliaukio was designed by Timo and Tuomo Suomalainen and consecrated in 1969. This captivating church is built into solid rock with unfinished granite walls and a rolled copper roof. You get the feeling that you are inside a modern artwork. Inspiring and energetic concerts are often performed here. At other times this is a wonderful place to sit and meditate and, of course, pray.

Puu-Käpylä is a neighborhood where you can wander around and take in the quaint beauty of early 20th century classicism. These houses, which were built in the 1920s and 30s, have been saved and beautifully preserved. This neighborhood is very popular among artists, writers and musicians.

There is plenty to see and do in Helsinki. You may want to visit an art museum, sit in a cozy café, sample Finnish cuisine, or stay out late in a nightclub. You can cruise on a boat around the archipelago, go sightseeing by bus, or see the places of interest on tram 3T. On the other hand, you may just want to stroll around the town keeping you eyes and ears wide open. That's a magnificent way to discover the real Helsinki.

You can view Finlandia Hall, created by Alvar Aalto, from the shore of Töölöbay.

The Word on Women

Tarja Halonen
Finland's President

Finnish women are seen by some as beautiful and intelligent. Others may find them cool and fickle. Still others may use descriptive words such as shy or tolerant or strong. It all depends on the who, where, why, how, and what. The two words "Finnish woman" bring different images to different people. The image that is NOT likely to appear, however, is repressed, inferior or uneducated.

In Finland's traditional agrarian society, women worked alongside men, often doing the same jobs while struggling to make ends meet. Finnish women had already gained many rights in the 19th century and, in 1906, they became the first in the world to be granted full political rights: both suffrage and eligibility to run for office. Women have exercised these rights enthusiastically over the years and a substantial number of them have been elected to public office.

In 2000, Tarja Halonen was elected President of the Republic, and at the time of this writing, the Speaker of the Parliament, the Mayor of Helsinki and a substantial number of government ministers are women.

Some milestones for women include: The Surname Act, permitting spouses to take the surname of either partner or to retain their original surname. The Equality Act, prohibiting discrimination by sex in the work place, as well as in other situations. The 1988 decision by the Evangelical Lutheran Church that allows women to enter the clergy. The amendment to the Equality Act in 1995 giving women the right to volunteer for military service.

Finnish women tend to be well educated and they make up a clear majority of undergraduates. Women dominate the humanities, whereas men are more concentrated in the fields of science and technology.

It is rare to find women who do not work nowadays, although you won't find total equality in working life. Women dominate in the fields of health care, social work, teaching and office work. They hold most of the leading positions in cultural life. The total number of Finnish women entrepreneurs is less than men, but they are at the forefront of design and other artistic fields.

Men tend to dominate in construction, highly skilled labor, business and management, although younger women are going into these fields more and more. At present women's overall salaries are around 80% of men's but this difference seems to be gradually changing. The future looks promising for Finland's females.

Now, about that description of Finnish women. Maybe we could call them strong but feminine, quiet but assertive, smart but modest... or maybe not, if they hear this kind of description, it might just go to their heads.

Significant Others

Swedish Tongued

Once upon a time, Finland belonged to the Swedish empire, so you probably can guess what the official language was. If you wanted to get anywhere in life in those days, you had to speak Swedish well. When Russia took over the helm of Finland, Finnish was given equal status with Swedish. Over the years, with the achievement of

independence and the Finnish nationalism movement, Swedish started to lose its popularity. Indeed, some people with Swedish last names went so far as to change them to Finnish ones.

In 1815, around 15% of the population spoke Swedish as a mother tongue, nowadays that figure is down to 6%. It still remains the second official language, though, and is carefully watched over by Swedish speakers and supporters of the language. There is even a Swedish People's political party.

Historically, much of the great poetry and prose was written in Swedish. The uppers classes, the intellectuals and the powerful used Swedish exclusively. Even today a large proportion of the politicians, leaders of business and big names on the cultural scene speak Swedish as a mother tongue. Every year a surprising amount of good Swedish-language books, films and theater productions find audiences among the general population of Finland. Swedish language newspapers, television shows, and radio programs continue to be popular. Swedish universities, institutions, and schools in Finland are known for their quality education and successes in job placement.

Some critics question the wisdom of requiring Swedish in both education and in many jobs, and they may have some valid claims. On the other hand, there is an overwhelmingly excellent reason for keeping the Swedish requirement: the eight million Swedes who live in the country next door! Not to mention the Norwegians and he Danes who speak related languages.

The Lapland Cowboys

The Sami (Lapps) are an indigenous people who reside in Finland, Norway, Sweden and Russia. There are 6,500 Sami living in Finland and most of them are located in northern Lapland. In Utsjoki they actually make up the majority. More than half of them speak Sami and they now have the right to conduct official business in their own language and around 600 pupils are presently studying in Sami.

The Samis' conventional means of livelihood include reindeer herding, fishing agriculture and forestry. Tourism has given a boost to the Sami traditional handicraft of wood, bone, antler, pelt and leatherwork, not to mention corny *T-shirtwork*. In exchange for currency they will happily take visitors on dogsled rides, nature walks or invite them to reindeer farm cultural evenings that include lots of singing, celebrating, eating and beer drinking in the Sami version of a teepee. And please pass the reindeer milk.

The literature, art, music and theater of the Sami have greatly enriched the culture of Lapland and made positive contributions to the diversity in the whole country. *Yoiking*, a chant based on a special vocal technique, can be heard at various cultural events around Finland. Many young people appreciate modernized yoiking with guitars, drums and other instruments. Will "heavy metal" and "hip-hop" *yoiking* be next?

Undeniably, these indigenous people have made progress toward restoring their identity. They have a national anthem called "The Song of the Sami," their own parliament and their own flag. They also wear colorful national costumes with pride. But please, don't you wear one. The costume looks chic on Samis, but ridiculous on tourists. All right, you can buy the hat.

The Tango Kings

The first Romanies (Gypsies) came to Finland in the 16th century and today they number around 6,000. Romanies belong to tribes called *cherhas* and these are divided into extended families. Behavior of the families is carefully supervised with older people in the dominant roles. The women often wear highly decorated, petticoated, festive dresses while the men usually dress in more somber attire.

Romanies have traditionally worked as horse traders, craftsmen, artisans, entertainers and fortunetellers. Many of these vocations were lost when Finland became an industrialized nation and this has brought difficulties to Romany communities. Efforts to help Romanies adapt to the current employment situation have met with some success but there are still many problems. More effective training and educational programs will be needed in the future.

Some Romanies have succeeded as entrepreneurs and small business owners. Others have done well as singers and actors. That old, ever-popular favorite, the Finnish tango, wouldn't be the same without all the golden-throated Romany chanters bringing sweet melancholy to the audiences. *One summer night....*

10 Reasons to Visit...

Turku

1. **Turku Castle** – An impressive gray stone castle dating back to 1280. It houses a historical museum containing many of Finland's national treasures. Here you can partake of a genuine medieval feast.

2. **Luostarinmäki Handicrafts Museum** – When the Great Fire of 1827 destroyed most of Turku, Luostarinmäki was spared, and today it is preserved in its original condition. Wander among thirty workshops from the pre-industrial era.

3. **The Sibelius Museum** – Contains collections relating to the great composer, Jean Sibelius, and hundreds of musical instruments from all over the world.

4. **"Ett Hem" Museum** – The elegant home of Consul Alfred Jacobsson and his wife. It is preserved in its original condition as a fine example of upper class life in Turku at the turn of the 19th century.

5. **The Christmas City** – From Advent on December 3rd to *St* Knut's Day on January 13th, the banks of the Aura River are beautifully illuminated. During this period Christmas traditions of olden times,

concerts, exhibitions, special events and Christmas tours grace the city.

6. **Moominworld** – An island theme park, located in nearby Naantali, which celebrates the characters from the stories of the beloved children's author, Tove Jansson.

7. **The Archipelago** – The islands surrounding Turku are one of Finland's greatest attractions. There is a rich choice of sea vessels offering tours around this breathtaking seascape.

8. **A Promenade Along The Aura River** – This is probably the best way to get acquainted with Finland's oldest city. You can wander along the banks anytime of year, choose your own pace and stop often to admire the sights.

9. **A Theme Night Out** – Have a night on the town with a difference. There's the Old Bank, an English-style bar-restaurant in a converted bank; the Pub Uusi Apteekki, a former pharmacy; the Brewery Restaurant Koulu, formerly known as Cygnaeus School; and Restaurant Puutorin Vessa, located in a building that was a public lavatory for fifty years.

10. **Aboa Vetus** – The museum is actually a medieval town block that was discovered by accident during renovation work several meters below ground. Here you can stroll around in antiquity.

Tampere

1. **Walk Along The Tammerkoski Rapids** – Get a good look at the historic and cultural center of the city. Admire the rushing waters and visit some of the restored old factory buildings along the way.
2. **Pispala** – A unique, hillside neighborhood where wooden houses were lovingly built by a community of carpenters, bricklayers and other craftsmen. This residential area has long been a source of inspiration for writers and artists.
3. **Särkänniemi Adventure Park** – This amusement park includes action-packed rides, a dolphinarium, a planetarium, an aquarium, a children's zoo, and the Sara Hildén Art Museum. Also, inside the park you can take a lift to the top of Näsinneula, Finland's highest observation tower.
4. **Vapriikki Museum Center** – Housed in the historical factory milieu of Tampella Mill Shop, Vapriikki features themes from archaeology to

The Tammerkoski Rapids

modern art, and from handicrafts to technology and nature. The collection consists of 350,000 items.

5. **The Spy Museum** – Here you can find out about lie detector tests, bugging devices, deadly umbrellas, and famous spies. The collection includes special weapons, spy cameras, encryption, radio technology and other devices essential for a respectable secret agent.

6. **Outdoor Concerts** – In the summer, enjoy choir and ensemble music on Tuesdays and Thursdays, and folk dances on Wednesdays in the park by the old library. Free entrance.

7. **Tampere Film Festival** – An internationally recognized venue featuring short films and animations by distinguished directors. The atmosphere is relaxed and fun.

8. **Viikinsaari** – An island paradise of historic buildings, beaches, playgrounds, sport fields, miniature golf, an open air theater and a diverse program of activities. You can also barbeque, take a lakeside sauna, rent a rowboat and dance to live music.

9. **A Lake Cruise – Tampere** has an ample choice of regular cruises to various destinations as well as charter boats for hire. Most vessels have decent restaurant services and are fully licensed to serve alcoholic beverages.

10. **Pyynikki** – The world's highest ridge is an outdoor recreation area set amidst forest and water. For a magnificent view you can visit the Observation Tower, and maybe try one of their famous doughnuts.

Lahti

1. **Harbor Area** – Sit at a café on the waterfront boulevard enjoying the picturesque scenes of steamships, motorboats and sailboats plying the blue waters. Visit the fish market, the village market, the artesian shops, the galleries, or just watch the people moving about this intimate place.

2. **Sibelius Hall** – This acoustically outstanding hall is the largest wooden building constructed in Finland for a hundred years. A wonderful place to attend a concert by the internationally famous Lahti Symphony Orchestra and to eat a fine meal.

3. **Musical Fountain** – The biggest fountain of its kind in Scandinavia, where water, music and colored lights combine to create an enchanting symphony.

4. **Lanu Sculpture Park** – Set in natural surroundings, 12 sculptures of reinforced concrete depict human figures and themes of nature.

5. **Ski Jump Lookout Point** – A chair lift carries you to the base of Lahti's highest ski jump. Then take an elevator to the covered lookout point at the top.

6. **Ski Museum** – Find out about the history of skis and skiing from the ancient past to the present. In the interactive section, you can try a ski jump simulator, an artificial cross-country ski trail, laser rifles, and a slalom device.

7. **Radio and TV Museum** – Learn about the development of radio and TV technology during the past century. Listen to old radio programs, make your own programs with special sound

effects, shoot a film, perform in a TV program in the museum's own studio, and get acquainted with Data TV.

8. **Fishing Park Vonkale** – Go fishing the easy way at Lake Pikku-Vesijärvi. Here you'll find a fishing kiosk with equipment rental, a beach terrace, angling piers, and a fish well. The smoking of fish and catering are available to lucky fishermen.

9. **Kick Sledding** – How about trying an organized safari based on this unique sport?

10. **Hollola** – At this nearby community, you can visit the Pyhäniemi Manor House, which is one of the most appreciated examples of manor houses in Finland. A short distance away stands the stone Hollola Church, which is definitely worth seeing from both the outside and inside.

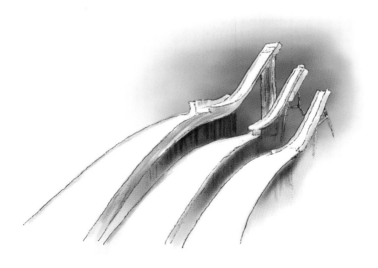

Oulu

1. **Tietomaa Science Center** – Science for the whole family. Whether you are fascinated by history, current events, sports, the future, or technology, you'll find something remarkable among the 200 devices and exhibitions. Additionally, there is the Super Screen featuring IMAX documents from around the world.

2. **Rotuaari** – Get acquainted with the center of the city by strolling on this pleasant pedestrian street. You'll pass the market place, boutiques, department stores, cafés and pubs. You'll probably end up making a few stops along the way.

3. **Beaches** – There are 17 official swimming beaches in Oulu where you can enjoy a refreshing swim or an uplifting sunbath.

4. **Marathon Ice Angling Competition** – On April 5–7 around 500 fishing enthusiasts try their luck for 48 hours. That's a lot of fish being pulled up through the ice.

5. **Turkansaari Open-Air Museum** – A folk museum displaying old rural buildings including a wooden

chapel from 1694, plus a forest and logging museum. There are tar burning, log rolling and handicraft demonstrations as well as folk music and folk dancing.

6. **Oulu Cuisine** – *Rieska,* salmon soup, blood pudding, vendace, bread cheese are some of the local specialties. You can sample them in the market hall or at the market place.

7. **Oulu Cathedral** – A grand, yellow, empire-style church that was designed by the renowned architect, C.L. Engel. Inside, in the vestry, you will find Finland's oldest portrait dating from 1611.

8. **Sailor's Home Museum** – Located on Pikisaari Island, it is the oldest house in Oulu. It was built in 1737 and was the former residence of a local sailor.

9. **Oulu Art Museum** – A place to contemplate the excellent, revolving exhibitions of international and Finnish art, and to enjoy the rich permanent collections. Moreover, the renovated former factory complex is a work of art in itself.

10. **Oulu University Botanical Gardens** – Beautifully landscaped with thousands of exotic plants. The tropical ones are located in a pair of greenhouses affectionately named Romeo and Juliet.

Kuopio

1. **Puijo Tower** – From the top of this tower you can view the endless mosaic of blue lakes and green islands. A revolving panoramic restaurant serves provincial specialties during the summer.
2. **The Marketplace** – Situated in the heart of Kuopio where you can experience the traditional, local atmosphere. Stalls offer a variety of fresh produce, beautiful handicrafts and *kalakukko* fish pies, the best-known specialty of the region.
3. **The Orthodox Church Museum of Finland** – Features precious gold and silver objects, lavishly embroidered church textiles and a magnificent collection of valuable icons.
4. **Kuopio Dance Festival** – Invades the city for a week of first-rate Finnish and international dance performances. You can also participate in one of the many dance courses on offer.
5. **A Tour of the Ironworks in Northeastern Savo** – The ironworks of Säyneinen shore, the bell foundry of Juutila, and the ironworks community in Juankoski depict the process of making iron from lake ore, and the passing down of traditional metal casting skills to the present day. In addition, you can get a look at life in both the ironmaster's manor and the workers' quarters.
6. **The Wine Information Center** – Provides information on berry and fruit based alcoholic products and manufactures a wide variety of berry wines, liqueurs and spirits. How about taking home a crowberry wine?

7. **For Animal Aficionados** – A number of farms in the region welcome those interested in getting acquainted with their domestic animals. At Kuopio Animal Park you can encounter over 200 animals representing 30 species. Just say, Quack, oink, moo, bow-wow, *baaaahh*...

8. **Bird watching** – Lake Maaninkajärvi, Lake Ruokovesi, Lake Patalahti and the Lapinjärvi Lakes are dream settings for ornithologists. Many rare species have been spotted and you may be lucky enough to add a white tailed eagle to your notebook.

9. **Hiking** – The Kuopio area is ideal for walking and rambling, with places to stop off for a picnic or to build a campfire. Puijo-Antikkala Nature Trail, Neulamäki Nature Trail, Kurhosaari Island Nature Trail and River Palosenjoki Route, are all moderate in difficulty. For a more challenging outing, you may want to take the route over the ridges in eastern Kuopio, which continues for 25 km.

10. **The Old Kuopio Museum** – A block of wooden buildings in the center of Kuopio with interiors of family homes and workshops from the 19th century to the early years of the 20th century. There is also a chemist's shop and a room once used by the prominent writer, Minna Canth. An exhibition room displays photos of old Kuopio.

Northern Exposure

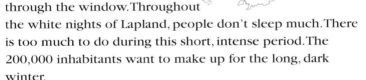

Lapland accounts for about one third of Finland, but probably contains most of the mosquitoes. It is called "Land of the Midnight Sun" because the sun never goes down during the summer. It's amazing to see people cuddling romantically at midnight in a dance restaurant with bright sunshine pouring in through the window. Throughout the white nights of Lapland, people don't sleep much. There is too much to do during this short, intense period. The 200,000 inhabitants want to make up for the long, dark winter.

The capital and only real city of Lapland is Rovaniemi, a charming, little town that serves as a gateway to the rest of the province. Rovaniemi certainly has its share of museums and sights but not to be missed is Arktikum, a science center and museum focusing on the Arctic regions.

Lapland is mostly a vast wilderness, and the picturesque landscape is covered with forests, tundra, fells, valleys, rivers, lakes and signs directing you to souvenir shops. It is an ideal place to go trekking and "get away from it all," but

Lapland is also a place where you can easily get lost, so you had better bring along good maps, a compass and proper clothing, or your getaway might be permanent. There are nature reserves and national parks where you may get a glimpse of a bear, a fox or an eagle. Or, according to legend, you might come upon a witch, wizard or spirit who may threaten you with evil powers. If this happens, just ask them to pose for a photo and they will disappear immediately.

The Sami (Lapps) are the indigenous people of Lapland. Their culture and language had been gradually disappearing, as the Sami assimilated into the more dominant Finnish and international cultures. Recently, however, there has been a revival of the Sami, and you can see them in Northern Lapland in their brightly-colored costumes herding reindeer, building traditional dwellings, or racing around in the latest model snowmobiles.

With 200,000 reindeer roaming around Lapland, it is no wonder that reindeer meat dishes are widespread. The meat has a wild taste and does not need much flavoring (hold the ketchup, please). Reindeer meat is healthy, low in fat and rich in vitamins and minerals. You can find reindeer served as stew, as steak, as chops, in salad, on sandwiches, as soup, as meatballs, as burgers, sautéed, roasted, cold smoked and end up eating it until you are ready to grow antlers.

In winter it is dark, cold and bleak in Lapland, which seems to attract a lot of people. This is the time to observe the spectacular aurora borealis, or northern lights. These dancing green, white or red lights are fantastic – and hopefully you are seeing the real thing and not just hallucinating from the cold. During Christmas charter flights from all over Europe and the world come into Lapland for a "Santa Claus" package.

In spring, it gets warmer and lighter, and Lapland is an outstanding place to go skiing. You might drive a snowmobile, go sledding or try ice fishing. You could also go on a dog sled ride, experience a reindeer safari, or on a warm day, have a picnic in the snow.

During the short summer, the weather turns pleasant and Lapland is full of adventurous tourists discovering the secrets of nature, enjoying fine views from the fells (the highest is Halti, 1,328 meters) or rafting down the rapids of a swift flowing river. This is also the time when optimists try their luck panning for gold.

A wonderful season to visit Lapland is during the early autumn when the leaves turn spectacular shades of red, yellow and gold. The weather is usually mild and the

The spectacular aurora borealis

These dancing green, white or red lights are fantastic.

mosquitoes have already died off. The forests are full of cloudberries and choice mushrooms. The Finnish name for this special period is *ruska*.

Lapland is the home of Santa Claus and he lives in a mystical place called Korvatunturi. His elf helpers these days are secretaries, shop clerks, marketing managers and computer operators. His village is located on the Arctic Circle where you can purchase jewelry, quality-made *puukko* knives, carved wooden bowls and T-shirts that say "I Love Lapland" on them. Not far away is Santa Park, his very own theme park. Santa is very friendly and speaks English well, and he is always happy to hear from his fans. If you would like to write to him, the address is: Joulupukki, 96930 Napapiiri, Finland or go to his website at www.santaclaus.posti.fi.

The Autonomous Islands

Åland holds a unique position in Finland. Due to a decision in 1921 by the League of Nations, this province of 6,500 islands (65 islands are inhabited) has political autonomy and is demilitarized. Åland has its own provisional government and flag, controls its own radio and television services, alcohol policy, child benefits, and agriculture. It is the only region in Finland that doesn't have two languages. They speak Swedish, but tourists can get service in Finnish, Swedish, English or German – provided they ask nicely.

The capital of Åland is Mariehamn, where about half the province's 26,000 residents live. It is an idyllic maritime town filled with charming buildings, gardens and greenery... well, okay, there are a few tacky tourist shops, too.

The islands are flat and distances are short. That makes Åland an ideal place for cycling, golf, horseback riding, camping and fishing. Going hiking gives a visitor the opportunity to enjoy the plethora of colorful flowers, the many varieties of bird life and the occasional deer. And to make things more exciting, there are some poisonous snakes and disease-carrying ticks scattered around.

The islands are flat and distances are short. That makes Åland an ideal place for cycling, golf, horseback riding, camping and fishing.

Turku

Island highlights include a game safari, the Maritime Museum, the Pommern Museum ship, the Hunting and Fishing museum, or perhaps you'd like to take part in a snail safari. Traveling around the islands you can observe some of the 16 medieval stone churches, the Castle of Kastelholm, protected forests, pristine beaches, rustic farms and captivating villages. And you certainly want to try the special black bread, pancakes with stewed prunes and cream, or at least sip on some locally produced apple wine.

If you happen to be a philatelist, you're in for a treat. Åland's exquisite stamps have attracted customers from over 100 countries. All of the stamps have a clear connection to Åland's history, culture, nature, society and autonomy, and are designed by local artists.

After a hard day of sightseeing, fishing or sunbathing, you might want to relax at one of the local restaurants and eat the local fish specialties, drink the local spiced liquor and practice some Swedish with the locals. Well, at least you can say, "Skål."

Going Fishing

Because of all its lakes, ponds, rivers, rapids, streams and sea, Finland is an excellent place to fish. Here you can catch perch, cod, pike, flounder, whitefish, pikeperch, rainbow and brown trout, sea trout, and salmon. But the main point is not how many fish you catch or how big. It's an opportunity to relax and enjoy the pure natural beauty of this country... while thinking up a good fishing story.

Every fisherman over 18 must have a fishing permit issued by the state, available at the post office. An exception is angling with a pole and line. If you don't use a reel, you don't need a fishing permit.

In addition, a local fishing license or permission from the owner of the waters is required. This can usually be arranged at the local tourist office. After that, you can get fishing information at a tackle shop, or better yet, ask around at the local bar.

For the rugged and warm-blooded, winter ice fishing can be a rewarding experience. You'd be surprised what people pull up through the ice, especially in northern Finland.

Ice fishing can be very pleasant when the sun is shining and reflecting off the ice. But sitting on the ice for a long period can also be a chilling experience, so you'll notice that veteran fishermen carry hot coffee, soup, or, very frequently, schnapps with them to help "thaw" themselves out.

Fishing is quite an amazing sport in that it makes the normally honest Finns into pathetic liars. Just listen to their unbelievable stories about how big and how many and what kind of a fight a certain fish put up. And remember, you will be expected to come up with your own exaggerated tales.

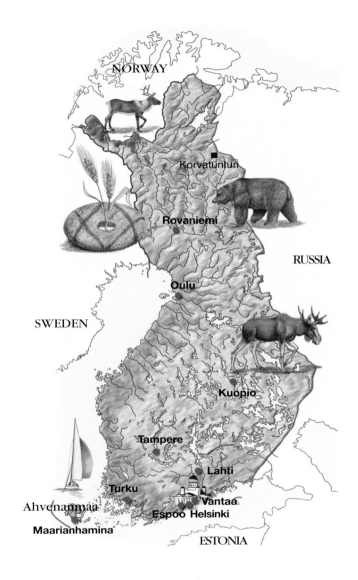

NORWAY

Korvatunturi

Rovaniemi

RUSSIA

Oulu

SWEDEN

Kuopio

Tampere

Lahti

Turku

Vantaa

Ahvenanmaa

Espoo Helsinki

Maarianhamina

ESTONIA

Finnish in Two Minutes

Finnish is one of the most beautiful
languages in the world... at least that's
what a lot of Finns claim. They will also tell
you that Finnish in not really difficult because,
unlike other languages, it clearly follows the grammar
rules. That may be true, but what they don't tell you is:
Finnish has more grammar rules than any other language on
earth. Anyway, after years of living in this country, I can
finally say, with confidence, that when a Finn asks me if I
can speak Finnish, I can immediately switch to his language
and produce intelligent conversation. After which, he will
smile politely and say, "It's so nice that you can speak our
language so well. "Then he will continue the conversation
in English.

Nonetheless, my point is that anyone can learn a few
phrases, and with the help of a Finnish colleague or two,
and a few beers, you can even pronounce them.

Good morning	Hyvää huomenta
Good day	Hyvää päivää
Good evening	Hyvää iltaa
Good night	Hyvää yötä
Good bye	Näkemiin
Yes	Kyllä

No	Ei
Maybe	Ehkä
Please	Olkaa hyvä
Thank you	Kiitos
No, thank you	Ei kiitos
I'm sorry	Anteeksi
Help!	Apua!
Do you speak English?	Puhutko englantia?
I don't speak Finnish	En puhu suomea
My name is	Nimeni on...
I'm in exports/imports	Olen vienti-/tuontialalla
I'm a sales manager	Olen myyntipäällikkö
Where is...?	Missä on...?
How do I get to...?	Miten pääsen...?
Where can I change money?	Missä voin vaihtaa rahaa?
What's the exchange rate?	Mikä on vaihtokurssi?
How much does that cost?	Paljonko tämä maksaa?
It costs	Se maksaa...
That's too expensive	Se on liian kallis
Breakfast	Aamiainen
Lunch	Lounas
Dinner	Illallinen
Can you recommend	Voitko suositella
...a restaurant where they serve	ravintolaa, jossa tarjoillaan
international cuisine?	kansainvälistä ruokaa?
...where I can find	missä tarjoillaan aitoa
genuine local cuisine?	paikallista ruokaa?
Any cheap pizza joints here?	Onko täällä edullista pizzapaikkaa?
The bill, please	Lasku, kiitos

I have a hotel reservation .... Olen varannut huoneen

Do you have any rooms that .... Onko teillä huoneita,
joiden...

don't face that factory? .... ikkunat eivät ole
tehtaaseen päin?

Entrance .... Sisäänkäynti

Exit .... Uloskäynti

Gentlemen's toilet .... Miestenhuone

Ladies' toilet .... Naistenhuone

Out of order .... Epäkunnossa

Grocery store .... Ruokakauppa

Liquor store .... ALKO

Pharmacy .... Apteekki

On sale .... ALE

Do you sell English-language .... Myyttekö englanninkielisiä

newspapers and magazines? .... sanoma- ja aikakauslehtiä

Where can I buy souvenirs? .... Mistä voin ostaa
matkamuistoja?

Cashier .... Kassa

Lift/elevator .... Hissi

Telephone .... Puhelin

Bus/coach .... Linja-auto

Train .... Juna

Railway station .... Rautatieasema

Tram .... Raitiovaunu

Bicycle .... Polkupyörä

Airplane .... Lentokone

I'd like to find a nice café. .... Haluaisin löytää mukavan
kahvilan

Can you tell me where. .... Voitko kertoa, mistä

I can find a good pub?. .... löydän kunnon pubin?
Beer/wine/Finnish schnapps....... Olut/viini/Koskenkorva
Cheers. .... Kippis

10 Useful Websites about Finland

Http: virtual.finland.fi – General information about Finland operated by the Ministry of Foreign Affairs.

Http: www.helsinki-hs.net – The international edition of Finland's largest daily newspaper the Helsingin Sanomat.
Http: www.hel.fi/english – Operated by the city of Helsinki, provides tourist and services information.

Http: www.mek.fi – Tourist information about the whole country. Operated by the National Tourist Board.

Http: www.finnair.fi Operated by the national airline, Finnair, concerning flights, hotels, and destinations.

Http: www.kulttuuri.net – Provides information about museums, happenings, concerts, and cultural events.

Http: www.mol.fi/migration/pateng.html – The official site for foreigners working in Finland.

Http: www.festivals.fi – Provides links and information about the largest festivals in Finland.

Http: tilastokeskus.fi – Provides statistics and facts about Finland and Finnish society.

Http: www.yle.fi – The home site of the Finnish Broadcasting Company.

THE AUTHOR

Russell Snyder, a native of California, has always been interested in other cultures. At the tender age of 21, he took a 44-day trip to Europe hoping to satisfy his travel lust. That only whetted his appetite. The next year he returned to Europe and backpacked around for six months. The year after that, he made a 6-month journey around the world.

Snyder studied Spanish one summer in Mexico and found he loved mingling with the people and getting to know their culture. He felt the same enthusiasm when he later worked in the Caribbean, France and Germany.

In 1982 he moved to Finland. It was only meant to be a one year stay, but after all these years he is still here discovering interesting places to see, finding rewarding things to do and encountering fulfilling experiences.

He earns his living as a journalist, lecturer and author. You may contact Russell Snyder at rustysnyder@hotmail.com